SPEECH
COMMUNICATION
HANDBOOK

Donald Clint Streeter / *University of Houston*

SPEECH
COMMUNICATION
HANDBOOK

PRENTICE-HALL, INC. / ENGLEWOOD CLIFFS, N.J.

Speech Communication Handbook is the third edition
of the book formerly titled Speech Handbook,
2nd edition, by Harry Grinnell Barnes.

ISBN: 0–13–827709–5

March 28 78

Library of Congress Catalog Card Number: 79–39314

10 9 8 7 6 5 4 3

Printed in the United States of America

PRENTICE-HALL OF AUSTRALIA, PTY. LTD., Sydney
PRENTICE-HALL OF CANADA, LTD., Toronto
PRENTICE-HALL OF INDIA PRIVATE LIMITED, New Delhi
PRENTICE-HALL OF JAPAN, INC., Tokyo
PRENTICE-HALL INTERNATIONAL, INC., London

iv

Table of Contents

v

073341

Preface

The first edition of this text, *Speech Handbook,* was written in 1936 for the introductory course in speech at the University of Iowa. At that time, Dr. Barnes dealt with four fundamental processes of speech and eleven basic attributes of speech. He provided seventeen assignments so students could practice the principles. In addition, there were word lists to be used to improve articulation and pronunciation. I remember, when I was a teacher in the program, that we went over each assignment in class, but since the groups met only once a week, we spent most of our time hearing speeches. The emphasis was on providing practice in speech making.

In 1955 Barnes began a revision and expansion of the text. He wanted to add a section on reading aloud, including some material for sight reading. After his death I continued the work, following his plans. The emphasis in the second edition was still on providing opportunities to practice—now both speaking and reading aloud.

In the last ten or twelve years many introductory courses have minimized speech performance in favor of lectures about and discussion of communication theory. *Speech Communication Handbook* contains new material on theory, but it remains performance-oriented. There are now seven sets of assignments and projects: one set in the field of rhetorical criticism of speeches in a cultural context, another set for students in business and the professions, and a third set for short occasional speeches have been added to the assignments from former editions on the speech inventory, the skills of speech making, the skills of reading aloud, and the long speech or reading.

Thousands of students have used *Speech Handbook* in the more than thirty-five years it has been available. I have taught hundreds of them in introductory speech courses in high schools, colleges, and universities and in short courses offered in the training programs of some corporations. This edition includes many of the text materials I have needed in my many years of teaching students to become more effective communicators.

Donald Streeter
University of Houston

SPEECH

COMMUNICATION
HANDBOOK

YOUR SPEECH INVENTORY

I A Speech Inventory—Why?

One of the wise practices of modern educational methods is to begin a course "from where the students are now." We may not like where they are. We may wish they were much more able than they are. We may even think they will never do the work of the course. Whatever we think, we should begin, with any particular class, from where they are now.

And so it is with this course. We need to take inventory of your needs and abilities. We want to know where you are now in your progress toward speaking effectively.

Experienced teachers will pretty well know "where you are now." They know about how much experience a class like yours has had and about what the inventory will show. But *you* need to know something about it too. Therefore, we will find out where you stand and go on from there. The assignments in this book are built on the inventories of many hundreds of students. It is likely that yours will show many of the same strengths and weaknesses that the others have shown. But we need to find out again, from *you*. We need to know *you*.

Remember that *you,* the speaker, are not exactly like any other speaker in any other class. As you participate in the work of this class you will get to know your classmates better than you will in nearly any other course, and they will come to know you equally well. It is you as a person that we will get to know.

2 What Does This Inventory Include?

This inventory includes many of the things that we believe are important to know in order to help you get the most benefit from this course. These things include a little about your personal background and examples of your speaking and reading aloud. There are six steps in this inventory: (1) your background; (2) the basic behaviors; (3) the essential skills of speech making; (4) the essential skills of reading aloud; (5) phonation; and (6) articulation.

Your Background—It makes a difference who you are. Some people have a background that may already have helped them become better speakers than others may ever become. Some may have a background that has hindered their making progress in speech making. You and your instructor should understand the parts of your background that might help you become a better speaker.

Please turn to the inventory assignments in Section 31.

The Basic Behaviors of Speech—When you speak, under any circumstances, whether in public or in private conversation, you have ideas, you formulate them through the use of words into thought units (usually sentences), and you express them through the activity of the nerves and muscles of your body. This action results in vocal tones, speech sounds, and bodily movements. For convenience of study, these actions are classified as follows:

Adjustment to the speaking situation—This involves the management of the functioning of your entire bodily mechanism during speech. Speakers who are not well adjusted to the speaking situation may be ill at ease, unnatural, tense, nervous, hesitant, uncertain, or unable to speak coherently. The well-adjusted speaker, on the other hand, is likely to be poised, natural, and calm, and to speak directly to his listeners.

Formulation of thought—Single words and words arranged in thought units, as used by the speaker, are the basis for creating in the mind of the listener the ideas that the speaker has thought or is thinking. Inadequacy in this activity is evidenced when the speaker's continuing thoughts are unrelated, interrupted, or inconsistent; when his statements are ambiguous, obscure in meaning, inexact, incomplete, or ungrammatical; when his vocabulary is limited, inaccurate, or inexpressive; or when his pronunciations are noticeably incorrect or inaccurate, often showing a lack of familiarity with the words he is using. Excellence here means that the speaker's thoughts are related, that his statements are clear and exact, and that his vocabulary is better than ordinary "hall-talk."

Phonation—This includes the production and variation of tones of the voice and their pitch, intensity, duration, and quality, through which the speaker expresses variations in meaning.

Pitch refers to highness or lowness of tone.

Intensity refers to loudness of tone.

Duration refers to the length of time a tone lasts.

Quality refers to the individuality of the tone, its clearness, richness, and pleasantness.

Articulation—This involves the modification of tones of the voice in forming the speech sounds while speaking. Speech sounds consist basically of vowels and consonants, which must be formed in continuous series correctly, accurately, and fluently if the listener is to understand easily what the speaker is saying.

Now, turn to Assignment A-2 in Section 31.

Essential Skills of Speech Making—Occasionally, we find it necessary to speak in public. Public speaking requires the exercise of certain skills which go beyond those used in conversing. These skills, for purposes of study, are classified as follows:

Choice of subject—Selection of a general topic or field of knowledge to talk about to a specific audience.

Choice of thought—The selection and statement of one specific phase of a subject that can be adequately covered in the time allowed.

Choice of material—The selection of experiences, illustrations, examples, anecdotes, facts, opinions, or quotations to develop or amplify the specific thoughts selected.

Organization of material—The arrangement of thoughts and materials in a manner and order best suited to secure and hold the attention of the listeners and to help them understand and remember what the speaker says.

Use of language—The selection of words and their arrangement into thought units to express the speaker's ideas.

Projection to the audience—The directness and enthusiasm with which the speaker presents and interprets the meaning of his thoughts. He must strongly stimulate the listener in order to gain and hold his attention and to cause him to respond appreciatively. The speaker's voice is important; his body must be alive with the full meaning—the ideas and feelings—of what he is saying to stir the listener to active participation in the situation and to insure complete and sympathetic understanding.

Control of bodily activity—Controlled posture, movements, and gestures while speaking. Such activity aids the speaker in focusing the attention of the listener on the ideas expressed. Bodily activity must be natural and must not call attention to itself. Some effective speakers use much bodily action; others use very little.

Rhythm—Fluency in speaking, suitable individual rate of speaking, appropriate changes in the rate of speaking, and the use of pauses without noticeable jerkiness, interruptions, repetitions, or hesitations.

Pronunciation—Choice of the proper speech sounds and their appropriate combination into syllables and words which are spoken correctly and accurately, with stress upon the proper syllables.

Voice control—Control of pitch, intensity, duration, and quality of voice in the expression of meaning, in relation both to the ideas expressed and to the understanding of the listeners. Not all speakers who project well control their voices well.

Next, see Assignment A-3 in Section 31.

Essential Skills of Reading Aloud—It is difficult to estimate the number of times one may read aloud in public. But think of the oral reading you have heard—secretary's reports, children's poems and stories at home, scripture lessons at church meetings, entertainers at club meetings, or speakers on radio and television. Although the skills required for reading aloud and for public speaking are basically the same, each represents a different type of skill requiring special study and practice. The basic skills in reading aloud are as follows:

Choice of material—The choice of a suitable selection for reading to a specific audience.

Arrangement of material—The use of an appropriate introduction and the use of appropriate transitional and connecting remarks to give unity to the material read. Arrangement includes cutting the selection if necessary.

Projection of thought—Interpretation of the thought content of the material to give a full understanding of its meaning to the listener.

Projection of emotion—Interpretation of the underlying spirit, mood, feeling, and emotional content of the material to insure an appropriate emotional response by the listener.

For control of bodily activity, rhythm, pronunciation, and voice control, see the corresponding sections above under "Essential Skills of Speech Making."

Now, please turn to Assignment A-4 in Section 31.

Phonation—This is the production of voice. We consider your voice as a part of your skills in the essentials of speech making and reading aloud. Now let us think of it for itself. There are four elements which distinguish your voice from all others: your *pitch* (the highness or lowness of your voice), your *duration* (the length of time you hold a tone), your *intensity* (the loudness of the sounds you make), and your *quality.* In order to identify voice qualities which are considered unpleasant or "unnatural," we use descriptive words such as the following:

1. Muffled—The tones and sounds seem to be produced in the throat. Make the sound *oo* as in the word "moot" several times. Then speak a sentence so that the tones of your voice sound as much as possible like *oo,* and you will have a sample of this type of quality. The tones seem to be throaty, dull, and indistinct.

2. Metallic—The tones and sounds seem to originate in the mouth. Make the sound *ee* several times. Then speak a sentence so that the tones of your voice sound as much as possible like *ee,* and you will have a sample of this type of quality. The tones seem to be thin, flat, and without richness; they sound high in pitch. They may carry well but are somewhat unpleasant to hear.

3. Nasal—Too much nasal resonance, because the breath stream is directed mostly through the nose, rather than the mouth. The sound you make has a "humming" quality about it, somewhat like the "ma-ma" sound of a talking doll.

4. Denasal—A lack of nasal resonance. For amusement, you can exaggerate this quality by making all *m* sounds as *b,* and *n* sounds as *d.* Thus "moon" becomes "bood." "Noon" becomes "Dood."

5. Harsh—A raucous, unpleasant, unmusical voice whose tones are more like noises. In pitch the tones may be high or low.

6. Hoarse-husky—A voice which sounds as some voices do during or following a severe cold.

7. Breathy—Breathing noises, as in exhalation, are heard above the vocal tone. The individual may try to speak as he is inhaling.

8. Infantile—A baby voice used habitually by one of high-school age or older.
Now, please turn to Assignment A-5 in Section 31.

Articulation—The production of speech involves breathing, phonation, resonation, and articulation. The last refers to the way you embellish your tones to form the identifying sounds of speech.
Finally, turn to Assignment A-6 in Section 31.

3 Now What?

Do you speak effectively? Few students do. The purpose of this course is to help you to achieve a style of speaking which is as *natural, correct,* and *effective* as possible *for you.* The pathways toward achieving this goal will vary with your needs and abilities, the condition of your speech mechanism, and the environment from which you have come. *In spite of limitations you can improve your speech.* There have been many instances of students who have become effective speakers in spite of initial inadequacies, poor equipment, and lack of experience.

The first step in improvement is for you to discover and recognize your needs and abilities as a speaker. We have tried to do this in the set of six items in your speech inventory. The second step is to become familiar with the goals you must attain and the pathways you must follow in attaining those goals. The third step is to supplant the old undesirable habits with new and more desirable ones through diligent practice and rehearsal before and after any speaking performance which you may have the opportunity for. Your instructor will set up speaking experiences for you which will direct you toward the goals you should try to attain. *You must do the rest through your own unstinted effort.*

In addition, you should take the opportunity whenever possible to hear good speakers and to speak frequently yourself. If you are thus stimulated by others and stimulate yourself, your improvement will be more effectively facilitated. The stimulation received from hearing or making a *good* speech may exercise subtle and unsuspected but nevertheless marked influences on your future performances.

The *first principle* for you to learn is that there are no rigid, hard, and fast rules for speaking at all times. The principles stated in the following pages are submitted as *wise principles* to be followed in most speaking situations. You have a greater chance of becoming a successful speaker if you follow them than if you do not. *When you have become an experienced speaker, astute in audience analysis, an authority on your subject, and confident of your success, you may do as you please, but you probably will not find it necessary to forsake the habits which practice in the use of these principles has engendered.* You may rest assured that they are sound. They have stood the test of time as well as the scrutiny of scientists and artists.

Recognizing Your Needs and Abilities—In the ratings your instructor made of your inventory performances, you will probably note more "4" ratings than any other. The reason is that "4" means adequate, and most people are about that.

Do not be surprised, however, if at the outset of this course you rate a "3" or a "2" in "Adjustment to the Speaking Situation" and "Formulation of Thought" (Assignment A-2), "Choice of Thought," "Organization of Material," and "Projection to the Audience" (Assignment A-3), and "Arrangement of Material," "Projection of Emotion," and "Voice Control" (Assignment A-4).

Most students have very little trouble with the production of vocal tones or an acceptable quality, pitch, intensity, and duration. But about 10 percent of you will have an articulation inadequacy of the type studied in Assignment A-6.

Goals in Improving Your Speaking Ability—This course is designed to help you improve. Three major parts of this handbook give detailed suggestions for improving the basic behaviors of speaking, the essential skills of speech making, and the essential skills of reading aloud. An understanding of these pages is part of your effort to set up goals for your improvement. Following this expository material are many assignments. Each is designed with a specific goal or aim in mind. And in the procedure for each, an accounting is made of what has been learned before. By studying the textual material and by working toward the aim of each assignment, you will work out your goals for this course as you go along.

Do not be impatient. You cannot become an opera singer in ten easy lessons. Nor can you become a great speaker in a first course in speech. As a matter of good advice, you should not set any such goal for yourself anyway. Be assured that you *can* improve, that you *will* improve, that you will be a more effective speaker after this course is over than you are now. Let that much be your goal for the time being.

Establish New Habits—Now, enjoy yourself with your class. If you have some ineffective habits of speaking, you will want to supplant them with new and better ones. From the sets of assignments in this handbook, you and your instructor may select those that seem to have the greatest promise for you. As stated before, it is likely that you will get to know your classmates better here than in nearly any other course you ever take—because whenever anyone gives a good speech, he tells a little bit more about himself, no matter what his topic.

II FOUR ASPECTS OF SPEECH COMMUNICATION

This handbook is designed to be used in speech-making classes carrying such titles as "Fundamentals of Speech," "Principles of Speech," "Business and Professional Speaking," "Principles of Speech Communication," "Public Speaking," or any other introductory course in speech making. It may be that those who take this course will never have an opportunity to take another speech course. They may never have a second chance to learn of the breadth of the field of speech.

These next few pages are addressed to those students. While the class spends several of the first meetings on the inventory assignments, they may read about the field itself.

What is the field of speech communication? A list of the areas of study might be grouped as follows:

Theory Regarding Communication
    Language Development
    Semantics
    Voice Science
    Phonetics
    Rhetorical Criticism
    The Process of Speech Communication
    Speech in a Cultural Context

Application of Theory
  Speech Making
  Interpersonal Communication
  Argumentation and Debate
  Oral Interpretation and Readers' Theater
  The Theater Arts
  Speech Communication on Radio and Television
  Listening

What to Do When Communication Breaks Down
  Speech Pathology
  Audiology

The two areas developed in this book are speech making and oral interpretation (reading aloud). There are sets of assignments in each area. A third area receiving some attention is interpersonal communication. There are assignments in discussion and the interview, but the attention paid to these activities is quite limited. This introduction to interpersonal relations in speech may prompt some students to go on to much more intensive study of the activity in another course.

To help the student of speech communication understand the field better, we shall now consider four topics: the process of communication, interpersonal relations, speech in a cultural context, and listening. They will help the student know how speech is a process, how it is auditor-oriented, and how it is a matter of interaction.

4   The Process of Communication

Until about twenty years ago, the textbooks in the field of speech concentrated on the speaker's activities in preparing and presenting a speech. The fundamentals often considered included:

Thought	Language	Voice	Action

When they discussed "thought," the writers spoke of "purpose" in speech: to inform, to persuade, or to entertain. They asked the speaker to consider his audience in selecting materials to fulfill his purpose.

Specialists began to work on the speech act. While their colleagues studied the history of rhetoric in the light of the classical canons:

Inventio	*Dispositio*	*Elocutio*	*Memoria*	*Pronuntiatio*
(Ideas and materials)	(Arrangement)	(Style)	(Memory)	(Delivery)

the scientists were saying that the act of transferring an idea from the mind of a speaker to the mind of a listener took place in five phases:

Psychological	*Physiological*	*Physical*	*Physiological*	*Psychological*
(Mind of speaker)	(Vocal mechanism)	(Air waves)	(Hearing mechanism)	(Mind of auditor)

Each phase of the act came under scrutiny. The more they speculated, examined, tested, and pondered, the more important the auditor became in the formula. They selected a name for the behavior which included him —communication. They labeled the area for study the "process of communication."

Models were conceived, arranged, and described to depict the act. A simple early model offered:

Speaker   Message   Listener

The speaker and the message are part of the same person. To reach the hearer, it was necessary to include:

Speaker   Message   Medium   Listener

Now the scientists concentrated on the process from its beginning to its end, and they realized that it has no end. It is a continuous, on-going thing. If you said it began with the speaker, you had to say it ended with him, because he received responses from his listeners, which in turn influenced the next thing he would say, and so on around and around. Thus the element of "feedback" came into focus:

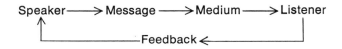

New terms were needed to identify what was being done. The first edition of this book, written in 1936, listed the four fundamental processes as:

Adjustment to the Speaking Situation
Symbolic Formulation and Expression
Phonation
Articulation

The word "encode" was selected around that time to identify the behavior of using symbols, as a companion word for "decode," which described the behavior of receiving sound symbols.

Many disciplines made their contributions to the study: psychology, linguistics, semantics, physics, pathology, and others.

Various models began to appear. They included such features as:

Source   Message   Channel   Receiver

At each point along the way, we were told, there can be a breakdown in the process. The start can be blocked if the source of the communication is unfamiliar with the culture in which the encounter with his receivers takes place, if he does not understand the social system, if his knowledge of what he wants to say is limited, if he does not know the symbols used by his hearers, or if he does not have the skills of communication necessary to send out his message on the air waves (for example, if his speech mechanism will not function properly—if the quality, pitch, volume, or frequency of his utterance is grotesque or if he is unable to articulate, enunciate, or pronounce understandably). What is more, if his attitude belies the meaning he intends or hopes to convey, a speaker's communication may be blocked at the start of the process.

His message may be garbled—if that is the word. The symbolic code may be foreign, the structure and syntax of his language usage may be distracting, the content may be inadequate for his purpose, or the elements of his discourse may be incomprehensible.

In the channel there may be too much "noise," as the scientists called it. Too many distractions through seeing, hearing, touching, smelling, and tasting other things can keep the message outside the ken of the receiver.

It may be that the speaker—how he looks or how he sounds—is his own worst distractor. Or it may be that the distance between speaker and receiver is too great. Or there may be interfering sounds.

On the other hand, the problem may lie with the listener. What if he comes from another culture or another social system, has no knowledge related to the message, or has attitudes which prevent him from decoding the message in an approximation of the one sent by the source?

All of these topics come under scrutiny in the study of the process of communication.

5   *Speech in a Cultural Context*

A man speaks to the people of his times on the problems of his times.

In this text we are much concerned with the audience. We analyze him, plan for his response, speak to him, and react to him. Such an attitude toward the listener has its roots in the history of man's communication. Speech instruction has paralleled the society in which man has lived; it has reflected his opportunity to speak to his fellow citizens. We shall see how well, as we take a brief look at the history of speech making, the role of the citizen in his society has influenced his need to speak, his right to speak, and his instruction in speaking.

Serious consideration was first given to a person's speaking ability 500 years before Christ. Long before that the Egyptian Ptah-Hotep had produced a book that gave speech-making instructions of a sort and the

Greek writer Homer had written some speeches and had attributed them to his heroes. But by 500 B.C., people in Sicily really needed to speak. There was a problem of land ownership and a man had to go before the courts to prove his proprietary rights. The times called for it, and Corax produced a book for the times—a book on persuasion, explaining the parts of rhetorical argument.

About the same time, or not long afterward, a number of Greeks taught men to speak up in their democratic society. Protagoras, Gorgias, and Isocrates, to name three of the most eminent, taught their pupils how to debate both sides of a question, how to develop a praiseworthy style in speaking, and how to make their speech elevated, noble, and educated. The times called for this type of speech and these teachers of rhetoric provided the instruction.

There was an opportunity for chicanery in teaching and practice, and there were teachers who taught the people rhetorical tricks. Plato denounced these Sophists, as they were called, and the opprobrium of his attack has stuck to this day. We use the word "sophist" now to characterize someone whose reasoning is captious, deceptive, or fallacious.

Aristotle followed with his *Rhetoric,* in which he systematically dealt with the speaker, with the audience, and with the speech. He identified the types of "proof" as *ethos, pathos,* and *logos* (character of the speaker, emotions of the listener, and result of logical treatment).

The democratic society of Athens flourished for hundreds of years and so did Aristotle's principles. Then Rome came to be the center of the civilized Western world. Although the public speaking of the ordinary man became less influential, the major orators still had their day. One of them, the great Cicero, wrote down his thoughts on rhetoric in several important books. He demanded that the speaker be a man of wide knowledge and express his thoughts in an elegant style. Quintilian, a transplanted Spaniard, taught in Rome at a time when there was little democratic participation in public affairs, yet he left us a great book, systematic and inclusive, offering a concept that we have come to revere: "A speaker is a good man speaking."

Then came the Roman Empire—a time of pompous display and democratic decay, which lasted for hundreds of years. The teaching of rhetoric came to serve merely the presentation of oratorical exhibitions. The Church was interested in training men for the clergy and the clergy distrusted the oratory of the day. Saint Augustine, however, presented a treatise in which he emphasized the Aristotelian principle that rhetoric proposes to make the truth effective.

As the secular schools developed during the Renaissance, they offered a curriculum which included rhetoric, but the instruction centered on the use of language.

By the eighteenth century the pendulum of man's participation in the affairs of his times had again swung toward democracy. In England men were once again allowed to speak out. The schools took up the challenge and taught speech making. Three great writers offered texts: Campbell, Blair, and Whately.

But, at almost the same point in history, just as these men were encouraging sound argument, direct communication, and appropriate and beautiful style, another group became prominent, influential, and imposing: the Elocutionists. Their emphasis was on delivery. Austin and Lovell, among them, went to extremes in teaching an artificial precision in voice and gesture.

By now, somewhat past the middle of the twentieth century, we have moved away from their influences, and we use the word "elocutionist" with a critical disdain.

The point we make here is that man is the product of his times. Man preserves his times or alters his times, but always speaks in his times. Great problems bring forth great speakers. Great speakers lead people in decision making. The people elect to office those who speak effectively. They choose for leaders of their service clubs those who speak well. They call on their fellows who are effective speakers to speak on hundreds of various programs. There is in man's speaking a cultural context, an environmental image, and a historical rhetoric. Man truly speaks in his times.

6 Interpersonal Speech Communication

The speaker, the message, the audience: these have long held a prominent place in our course work in speech. Our plans have been geared to helping the individual become a better communicator—to stand on a platform facing an audience, to present an uninterrupted speech, planned in its entirety and designed to meet the needs of the audience, and to anticipate the reactions and satisfaction of the audience.

But man's speech communication is not always like that. More often he is likely to be in a situation in which his speech is interrupted, in which the conclusion of the presentation is different from what he had planned, and in which the responses of his audience are frequent, immediate, and equal to his own in continuing the presentation. We are referring to the interpersonal speech communication situation, whether one to one or one among several.

It is not the purpose of this book to provide for many class assignments in the one-to-one speech situation, or the one-among-many situation. Such activities as the job interview, the office call, the personal conference, and the group meeting for discussion of policy, plans, or problem solution are important—so important that our speech departments devote entire courses to them—but not for our course. We are interested in the individual speaking to groups.

At the same time, to give some insight into the type of communication and the participation an individual may have, it is well to consider the interpersonal aspects as a type, a class, a form of speech communication.

The preparation for interpersonal communication is similar to that for individual performance. The topic is selected, the purpose is identified, the central idea is formulated, material is gathered, and the presentation is planned.

Comparable to the selection of a topic might be the decision as to the type of meeting—for example, a conversation between two members of a firm, a staff conference to consider a new directive, or a meeting of supervisors to identify a problem and seek solutions.

The central thought of a speech can be a definite statement. A group meeting, on the other hand, usually begins with a question.

Just as there is a pattern in the ordering of the main ideas of a speech, so there is a pattern in a discussion: identify the problem, describe its characteristics, point out its causes, set some goals, offer several possible solutions, evaluate the suggestions, and try to arrive at a mutually agreeable course of action.

But when we come to the matter of presentation, we note the differences. Whereas a speaker can chart his course from beginning to end, with a group anything can happen.

Interpersonal relationships lead to multiple barriers to communication. How frequently we misunderstand. How often we disagree. How many times we have different information, much of it faulty.

The part of the group leader can be described in terms of his duties: he introduces topics, he summarizes progress, and he directs the course of the discussion.

The participant in a discussion group has his own role to play. He should do his homework, offer his information at the appropriate moments, listen to the others, and cooperate in careful appraisal of the suggestions. The trouble is that the role he plays is more than just being another one in a group. He is an individual with a unique personality and he frequently represents a particular point of view. That is his role. He has status. The relationships among the members of the group are interpersonal ones. If the atmosphere is friendly, open, mutually trusting, and sincere in a search for a satisfactory conclusion, then much can be accomplished. If it is not such a productive climate, the leader will need infinite skill to keep the discussion on course, to encourage reluctant members to cooperate, to suppress the obstreperous members, and to arrive at mutual agreement without breaking up in confusion.

While you are in this course, you might try a job interview or two. Those in the same field of work might attempt a discussion aimed at solving a troublesome problem in the field. Do these things as an introduction to the activity of interpersonal communication. Perhaps you will understand its importance and want to learn much more.

7   Listening

Listening directs our living. Perhaps because it has seemed so obvious, we have not spent much time on it in school. The very study of speech has been considered in the same way: "Everybody speaks. Why should we study something in school that we have been doing all our lives?" "Everybody listens. If you couldn't listen you wouldn't know where to go. Why should we study listening in school?"

During the last twenty-five years, however, enough emphasis has been placed on listening to put it in our textbooks and in our courses of study. Researchers have asked so many questions about it: What is it? Is it important? Are there factors that influence it? Is it anything like reading? Can it be taught? Can it be measured?

Listening has been identified as important in man's life. His use of language is dependent on it. As a baby he listens to and imitates what he hears. Thus is begun his comprehension of his human ability to formulate and express oral symbols.

In school the child listens for instructions and thereby learns to perform.

A person listens for entertainment. He listens for work assignments. He listens to doctors, to clergymen, to lawyers, and adjusts his living ways.

When conflicts develop and society resorts to discussion to settle its problems, he listens to grievances, offers solutions, listens to advocates, and decides on courses of action.

Listening accounts for a good deal of man's time. More than two-thirds of his waking hours are spent in some form of communication and just a little less than half of that time is spent listening.

We know a number of things about listening, now that we have given it our attention in recent years. We know that hearing and listening are not the same thing at all. It is easier to provide an example today than it was fifty or sixty years ago. Nowadays it is common for a person to have a radio or television going while he is doing something else. Fifty years ago a school boy or girl could not have had a record player or radio going as he studied. Today he can. It becomes "background music": he hears it, but he doesn't listen to it. Take another example: some offices and places of business have special types of background music played softly throughout the day. The workers hear it, but they don't listen to it.

What is it about listening that makes it important? First there is the desire of the one who hears. He must want to get the message. He can either turn it on or turn it off. He must want to turn it on. This we can teach our students. Listening calls for some effort on your part. You must want to get the message. In the speaking situation the speaker cannot do it all. You must help him by wanting to listen to him.

Next, what can the listener do to help get the message better—to help decode what the speaker says into understandings that approximate the thought the speaker had in mind as he was encoding? We tell him to listen for ideas, rather than facts. Facts slip out of memory much faster than ideas. Listen for ideas. Do not let your note taking develop into the listing of a lot of facts. They prevent your restructuring the ideas. Do not jump too quickly to a conclusion. Let the speaker develop his idea himself. Probably you can think a lot faster than a lecturer can speak, but hold with him. Don't daydream or go off on a tangent. Keep listening. Distractions may attract your attention. Learn to stay with the speaker. Let the noises become background, just as you have learned to let your radio play in the background without disrupting other activities—perhaps reading this book, for example.

On the day a listener says, "I don't believe it," he has taken the next step in the listening process. He has begun to evaluate what he hears. He has not just restructured and accepted. He has weighed the information and found that he cannot accept it at face value.

When asked why he does not believe it, he may answer, "I don't know why, but I don't believe it. I know the speaker is a man of great reputation. I know his personality is most attractive. He looks wonderful on the platform. But as I think about what he said, I must put aside who he is and what he is and conclude that he is outside his area of expertise. I just can't believe him. I need more evidence."

On the other hand, this cautious listener, who is skeptical of believing just because the speaker seems to be one who should be accepted because of who he is, might also look at himself, the listener, and say to himself, "Do I have some preconceived ideas about this subject that are influencing what I am hearing?" It is hard to disprove the old saying that "We hear what we want to hear." Our backgrounds and attitudes predispose us in certain ways. Good listening demands of us the difficult task of setting aside our attitudes as we evaluate what the speaker said.

One way to get at what the speaker really said is to examine his words. We know that a specific word conjures up different pictures in the minds of the different members of an audience. "State Park" may call up pictures of trout-laden streams to the angler, or of roads with no billboards to the beauty lover, or of miserable toilet facilities to the fastidious, or of crowds of yelling kids on holidays to others, or of rained-out picnics to still others. Listen to a speaker and try to determine *his* mental picture through the words he uses.

While you are about it, listening to his words, check him on his "propaganda." Does he resort to some of the techniques identified by the analysts as the "bandwagon" technique ("Try it—everyone else does."), the "hasty generalization" ("Look what happened here and here and here. Why, it's all over!"), the "glittering generality" ("Isn't it good, isn't it splendid! It's the American Way!")? There are many more: "name-calling," "plain folks," and "transfer," for example.

Finally, as a listener, you react. First you hear and restructure. Then you evaluate. And then you react.

Since we are interested in the whole process of communication we call your attention to the circular form of the model—the speaker gets feedback from the listener, which influences the rest of his speech. So, how do you want to react? It will influence the speaker in some way.

In our class we want the speaker to know that we are for him, that we want to help him to improve and become a better speaker, that we want the morale of the class to be high.

Students learn as they go through school how to smile and nod in approval at what a lecturer says—without really being "present" at all. Try to avoid that with your classmates. Don't, on the other hand, take the question-and-answer period as an opportunity to jump on everything your classmate has said in his speech.

Try not to go to sleep on your classmates. Don't read the college paper during speeches. Try not to frown or groan or fidget in annoyance.

Try your best to seem to be in communication. Look at the speaker's eyes so that he may look into yours when he has a chance. Sit in what might be called a receptive position. Can you give the impression that, if given the chance, you would be pleased to discuss the matter more fully, but if time does not allow, you can wait for another opportunity?

It is difficult to listen. But if you would have the speaker feel that his effort was worthwhile, you can do so by showing that you are listening, really listening.

*   *   *

These are thoughts to help acquaint you with the field of Speech Communication. We have considered the process of communication, speech in a cultural context, interpersonal speech communication, and listening. Your instructor may wish to lecture further on these concepts, or on others of his choosing. The class may decide to do oral reports or term papers on these topics or others. It is yours to decide. This handbook is designed primarily as a manual to assist you in preparing and presenting your speeches and oral readings.

III THE BASIC BEHAVIORS
   OF SPEECH

8 What Happens When We Speak?

The Speech Act—The term *speech* refers to the behavior or act of speaking. When normal, the act of speech is a total bodily response to a speaking situation of some kind. It is a single, coordinated muscular response to nerve impulses coming from the speaker's brain.

These nerve impulses occur as a result of thoughts and feelings which the speaker wishes to express in that speaking situation. His thoughts are expressed in words arranged in thought units and sentences. Each word is composed of selected speech sounds. Each speech sound evolves from the speaker's tone of voice at the moment. Listeners hear and react to the tone of his voice according to its pitch, intensity, duration, and quality. Appropriate variations in the pitch, intensity, duration, and quality of his natural tone of voice lend interpretation to his thoughts. Thereby, the listener becomes more fully aware of their logical and emotional meaning.

As the speaker formulates and utters his thoughts, natural bodily tensions, movements, and poses occur. As a result, the meaning and significance of his thought and feeling is more fully appreciated by the listener.

The Speech Mechanism—In speaking, the entire bodily mechanism is used. Certain parts of the mechanism, however, are especially important. They are: the breathing mechanism; the larynx containing the vocal folds; the cavities of the throat, mouth, and nose; the hard and soft palates; the tongue, the teeth, the lips, and the muscles of the face.

In a normal mechanism the teeth are properly occluded and free from spaces between them. The tongue is normal in size for the mouth cavity, neither too large nor too small, and comparatively free in its movements. The hard and soft palates are normally developed. The latter is active in narrowing and closing the opening between the nasal cavity and the throat. The lips are properly formed so that they can close firmly to stop the breath and release it quickly and explosively, as necessary. The facial muscles are normally developed and free from paralysis or inactivity.

The Functions of the Speech Mechanism and Other Bodily Parts

—To understand the functioning of the speech mechanism, it is especially important to note that, in addition to playing a vital part in the speech process, these parts of the mechanism have other, more important bodily functions to perform. That they exist primarily to perform these other bodily functions should be recognized. Speech has sometimes been called an "overlaid" or "usurped" function.

The main function of the *breathing mechanism* is to get air into and out of the lungs to sustain life.

The chief functions of the *larynx* (the *voice box*) are to regulate the supply of air entering the lungs and to prevent bits of food or other foreign particles from entering the trachea or windpipe.

The *tongue, teeth, lips, palates,* and *facial muscles* function primarily in the taking in, chewing, and swallowing of food. The *mouth, nasal,* and *throat cavities* are passages through which air enters and leaves the body. Food also passes to the stomach through the mouth and throat cavities.

Many normal and abnormal but primary activities of these parts of the mechanism interfere with the speech act. These include: inhalation, chewing, swallowing, sneezing, coughing, hiccoughing, sobbing, laughing, sighing, and yawning. If you are speaking, for example, and suddenly need to sneeze, you will sneeze rather than speak. The primary function of sneezing takes over the mechanism at that moment.

Since the parts of the speech mechanism have these other primary bodily functions to perform, speech is a secondary bodily function. The speech mechanism thus is subject to instability and must be kept under constant control by the speaker.

Nerves and Muscles Must Function as a Unit

—The neuromuscular (nerve and muscle) organization of the speech mechanism is very complicated. Many nerves share in carrying impulses to the muscle groups that are called into play when you speak. Not one muscle, but many cooperate in the speech act. The muscles are arranged in pairs, right and left, each being an exact copy of the other but reversed in position and action.

These pairs of muscles receive their impulses to act from several nerve fibers—the right from the left hemisphere of the brain, the left from the right hemisphere of the brain. Hence, for the speech act to be normal and at its best, nerve impulses and muscle actions must synchronize. They must operate together continuously. They must be integrated in their action. All muscles and nerves which participate in the speech act must function as a unit in perfect time order and balance. When this is not the case, speech inadequacies result.

What Happens When You Speak—As a result of conditions at the moment, you have thoughts and feelings to which you desire your listener or listeners to react. As you speak, these thoughts and feelings become meaningful to the listener through your words, tones, inflection, movements, gestures, and facial expressions. As you continue to express your thoughts and feelings, the following occur almost simultaneously:

1. Breath in varying degrees of pressure is sent up through your larynx.
2. Your vocal folds in the larynx adjust and readjust appropriately, modifying the outgoing breath into a series of breath waves.
3. Your throat, mouth, and nasal cavities and their openings assume (a) coordinately, (b) momentarily, and (c) successively appropriate sizes and shapes to receive these breath waves and to amplify or build them up into the required vocal tones.
4. Next, these breath waves are further modified by your tongue, teeth, facial muscles, and lips to form the necessary speech sounds.
5. The breath waves, as now modified, are sent forth from your mouth and nose as sound waves and are transmitted through the air. (You have seen the ripples that occur when you drop a pebble into still water. The sound waves coming from your mouth and nose spread through the air in somewhat the same way.)
6. While your voice mechanism is sending forth these sound waves to the ears of your audience, bodily movements, gestures, and facial expressions are causing variations in the light waves that reach the eyes of your audience.
7. As the sound waves strike the eardrums of your listener, they are changed, through the mechanism of his ear, into a specific pattern of nerve energy. As this pattern of nerve energy reaches his brain it becomes meaningful to him, subject, of course, to the limitations of the sound waves as received by him and his capacity to interpret their meaning.
8. The light waves received by the eyes of the listener are also changed to a specific pattern of nerve energy, which records an additional impression in his brain. The meaning of this impression is interpreted in relation to what he is hearing you say at the moment.
9. As a result of receiving these sound and light waves, the listener may exhibit behavior or specific reactions which you may observe and to which you may react as you speak.

Four Fundamental Behaviors—For purposes of study—training and retraining—the speech act is divided into four fundamental behaviors. These are:

Adjustment to the speaking situation
Formulation of thought
Phonation
Articulation

These behaviors are the foundation of all forms of speaking activity —from conversation to formal oratory. They are treated in detail in the following pages.

9   *Adjustment to the Speaking Situation*

Adequacy in formulation of thought, phonation, and articulation is dependent upon the degree to which the speaker is mentally and emotionally adjusted to the speaking situation.

If you are well adjusted to the speaking situation you will possess a stable, well-integrated bodily mechanism, and will exhibit poise, balance, ease, naturalness, and purposiveness. You will be free from inhibitions, bodily tensions, and mannerisms. You will speak coherently, fluently, and emphatically.

If you are not well adjusted to the speaking situation, you may possess an unstable, poorly integrated bodily mechanism; lack poise; be unbalanced, ill at ease, unnatural, tense, or inhibited. Your behavior may be purposeless. Uncontrolled bodily mannerisms may become apparent. You may be nervous, excited, frightened, hesitant, or uncertain, and thus be unable to speak coherently, fluently, and emphatically.

If you are not well adjusted to the speaking situation when you face it, if your bodily mechanism is unstable, the other fundamental processes will be affected. You will not, therefore, be able to speak well. The following suggestions may aid you in becoming well adjusted to the speaking situation.

Understand What Good Speaking Is—Remember that the function of the speaker is communication, not display; that the audience wishes to hear and understand the speaker's ideas rather than to watch him speak and be impressed by his technique and extraordinary skill. The latter are always less important than communication. Good speaking is neither mechanical nor artificial; it possesses a quality of *naturalness.* Avoid the attitude that there is nothing interesting or worthwhile for you to talk about. You need not always speak on serious or profound subjects; you need not always present them in a serious and profound way. Choose subjects about which you already know a great deal. Your words need not be long or unusual, your gestures need not be elaborate or rehearsed. It is not necessary to use a certain type of posture or special hand and arm gestures or to move about the platform methodically. You are not required to have a richly melodious voice that sings its words in perfect tone and cadence. Nor is it necessary for your pronunciation to be as fine as that of professional actors. You need not speak so fluently that there are no hesitations, repetitions, or uncertainties. Use that style of speaking which best accomplishes your purpose in the specific situation. There is no style of speaking suited to all occasions.

Understand the Nature of the "Speech Act"—As we said before, the speech mechanism is an unstable mechanism. You learn that, because of its very nature, it is subject to inconstancies. You also learned that the speech organs have more fundamental functions than speaking and that these more fundamental functions take precedence over the "speech act" in sneezing, coughing, or breathing, for example.

Furthermore, the speech act is influenced by bodily and emotional states or disturbances. The functioning of the speech mechanism is affected by fear, excitement, anger, joy, sadness, surprise, fatigue, and so forth. Manifestations of emotional or bodily disturbances during the speech act include: breathing irregularities; stiff, unnatural posture and movements; uncontrolled muscle trembling, such as knees knocking or hands shaking; interruptions caused by swallowing, laughing, sighing, yawning, or forgetting; frequent and prolonged hesitations; sudden and uncontrolled changes in pitch, loudness, rate of speech, and quality of tone; inaccuracy or indistinctness of the speech sounds.

You must and can learn through experience to keep control over your reactions to these various mental, emotional, and bodily states. Realize, however, that a perfect functioning of the mechanism during the speech act is not only rare but improbable. Even the best and most highly trained speakers experience some of the difficulties that you do.

Be Realistic About Yourself as a Speaker—You may make an improved adjustment to the speaking situation by adopting a realistic point of view toward yourself as speaker. Know yourself. Find out the facts about yourself as a speaker. Appraise your talents. Do not think you are better than you are, but do not minimize your abilities. After your instructor has made a diagnosis of your speech needs and abilities in terms of the fundamental processes and the basic essentials of effective speaking, study the diagnosis. Become familiar with your weaknesses or inadequacies as well as with your strong points.

Then face the facts about yourself as a speaker. Accept the description of your speech needs and abilities as evidence of your present level of ability and use it as a starting point for your training. Avoid worrying about speaking situations that you have not been called upon to face and forget past speaking experiences in which you have not been successful. Do not spend time daydreaming, wishing you were a better speaker than you really are, or pretending that you have acquired skills which in reality you have not. Instead, admit your inadequacies, but learn to emphasize your strong points and minimize your weaknesses. Succeed in spite of your handicaps. Accept criticism in a sincere, matter-of-fact way instead of feeling that you have been personally belittled. Remember that a recognition of your own needs is the first step toward improvement. Adopt the following point of view: "I may not be an excellent speaker. In the beginning I may be a poor speaker with inadequacies, but I shall constantly strive to communicate my thoughts and feelings to my audience as naturally and directly as I possibly can, despite my limitations. With experience, I know that I shall improve."

Let Individuality as a Speaker Be Your Goal—Strive to develop yourself as a speaker in terms of goals that are not only possible but probable for you to attain. Individuality as a speaker should be your first goal. Your heredity and environment have made you an individual. Be yourself! Do not try to copy exactly the style someone else uses; his style is *his* individuality expressing itself. Let *your* individuality express itself! There is no style of speaking that is suited to all persons; but, in developing your own style of speaking, do not ignore the principles of effective speaking about which you will learn in many assignments. Modify your own personal speaking style in accordance with them.

Make a Speech at Every Opportunity—Seek opportunities to speak before audiences as often as possible. The best way to improve your adjustment to the speaking situation is through experience in speaking situations—all kinds of them. You may find at first that it is not easy, but you will also find that with each successive experience it is easier, and soon you will begin to enjoy it. Speak about topics with which you are thoroughly acquainted, that arise out of your own background and experience. Sometimes you will be able to plan what you are going to say over a considerable period of time. At other times you will speak with little preparation. Whatever the circumstances, when the opportunity comes, *speak,* make your contribution. Concentrate on your ideas and what they mean, not on how you say them. You will find that it will be easiest, in the beginning, to recount experiences that you have had— easier for you because they are part of you and because the audience will be immediately interested. And make these talks short!

Do not expect to become well adjusted to the speaking situation immediately or be disturbed if your progress is slow and gradual. Set a series of goals for yourself that you can reasonably attain, so that you need not be dissatisfied or unhappy with your progress.

Believe that Stage Fright Is a Natural, Normal Reaction—Difficulty in adjusting to the speaking situation is most frequently caused by stage fright, but stage fright is the natural, normal attitude and reaction of the inexperienced speaker. If you are not an experienced speaker, you may feel nervous and uncertain about yourself and how well you will do. But you must recognize that experienced speakers have, through their experience, become poised and confident that they can adjust to nearly any circumstance that may arise in speaking situations. You too can attain this poise and confidence through experience in speaking. It takes longer for some speakers to acquire it than for others, but you must speak often and in many kinds of speaking situations. Some of the following suggestions may help you:

1. Speak on topics about which you are well informed or on experiences that you yourself have had.
2. When you know that you have to make a speech, prepare well. Think about the topic, make notes, say it over to yourself. Have the notes with you and use them if necessary.
3. If the speech conditions permit, introduce some object in the speech and talk about it and demonstrate it. Or plan to use a blackboard diagram, which you draw while talking about it.
4. Think about what you are going to say. Before you are called upon, say the first sentence to yourself. Repeat it to yourself as you go to the platform. As you take your position on the platform, say it to yourself again. Then take a deep breath, say, possibly, "Ladies and Gentlemen," say the prepared sentence aloud, and your speech has begun.
5. If you are excited and seem to tremble before being called upon, relax and breathe deeply to counteract the bodily tension.
6. If you feel weak when you get to the platform, lean against something. If your hands or knees tremble, touch them against the desk or lectern to stop the trembling, which, when stopped, usually does not begin again.
7. Move about the platform. Be active. Make yourself use gestures— any kind. An active body will help destroy the evidence of your fears and actually cause you to be more at ease.

10   Formulation of Thought

Formulation of thought refers to the act of creating, arranging, and expressing thought while speaking. As a speaker converses he creates ideas, chooses and arranges words in thought units and sentences for their conveyance, and utters them, all as part of one act.

The speaker who is superior in formulation of thought states his thoughts coherently in a form that is adequate and essentially correct. He knows exactly what he is going to say and says it with economy of words and good taste. His thought is continuous, uninterrupted, consistent, and logical. It is also clear, exact, and obvious. His vocabulary is broad. He uses simple, specific, colorful words. His sentences are grammatically correct and express each thought completely, exactly, and emphatically. His words are pronounced acceptably.

The speaker who is inadequate in formulation of thought may lack coherence and consistency in his thinking and may use bad and incorrect forms in expressing his thoughts. He gives evidence of not knowing what he is going to say or how he is going to say it. He seems confused and uncertain. His successive thoughts may be disjointed, unrelated, interrupted, repeated, inconsistent, illogical, contradictory, or without a single end or goal. His statements may be obscure, inexact, and indefinite in meaning. His vocabulary may be limited, too simple, dull, ambiguous, vulgar, or inexpressive. His sentences may be grammatically incorrect. His pronunciation may be noticeably inaccurate.

If you are no better than adequate in this process, you should aim to develop more skill in the formulation of thought. Skill in thought formulation gives "dignity" and "distinction" to the speech and the speaker. It is through effectiveness in the exercise of this function that you provide the basis for the projection of your ideas to your audience with precision, exactness, and emphasis.

Formulation of Thought and the Speaking Situation—Formulation of thought is most simply defined in terms of the informal, rather than the formal speaking situation. The informal speaking situation is characterized by conversation about or discussion of a subject by two or more interested persons, in which each makes a contribution as and when he desires. The formal speaking situation is characterized by the speaker-audience relationship, in which the speaker does all the talking for the benefit of the listeners. Thought, when expressed in either type of situation, should have a purpose in terms of and relevant to the situation at the moment of utterance.

For thought to be purposive in its creation the speaker must have a knowledge of the drift of the points brought out in the immediate discussion, a sufficient knowledge of the subject under discussion to make possible a contribution to it in the form of fact or opinion, an interest in the subject and the discussion accompanied by a desire to contribute to it, an interest in knowing more about the subject under discussion as expressed in related questions, sufficient adjustment to the situation for the formulation and expression of thought to occur at its best, and a realization that when thought is expressed it must be formulated so that the listener may comprehend it.

For thought to be purposive in its formulation, its expression must show that it is complete, that is, the expression of a thought once begun must be completed without digression or interruption. It must be consistent, that is, the expression of the thought must observe logical order, and the words must follow in sequence. It must not be contradictory. It must be continuous, that is, there must be no frequent interruptions, hesitations, and uncertainties resulting from not knowing what to say or what words to choose in expressing the thought. It must be coherent, that is, details must be combined into a related whole. It must be clearly and specifically stated and free from abstraction and ambiguity. It must be correctly stated and free from error in grammatical structure. And finally, for thought to be purposive in its formulation, the speaker should speak acceptably, that is, his pronunciation of the words in sequence must be adequate.

In the formal speaking situation the speaker must exercise greater skill in the principles mentioned above than in the informal speaking situation. He must show that he has a knowledge of and experience in public speaking. Surely he must be sufficiently well adjusted to the speaking situation to allow for normal functioning of the bodily mechanism, thus facilitating the formulation and expression of his thought.

I I *Phonation*

Characteristics—Phonation refers to the production and variation by the speaker of vocal tones—their pitch, intensity, duration, and quality. Pitch refers to highness or lowness of tone. Intensity is loudness. Duration is the length of time a sound lasts. Quality refers to the individuality of tone.

A speaker is superior in phonation when his voice has a basic quality that is clear, full, rich, resonant, mellow, pleasing, and beautiful. It is more often medium or low in pitch. It is legato rather than staccato. It has a reserve of intensity. It is flexible, recording easily and without apparent effort the broadest and most subtle changes in thought and mood.

Voice Inadequacies—In evaluating the speaker's phonation, the skilled observer looks for the following inadequacies.

Organic inadequacies—Included may be:

1. Malformation of the nose, mouth, or throat cavities and the larynx.
2. Obstructions in the cavities, such as adenoids.
3. Chronic inflammations in these cavities and the larynx.

Pitch—Among possible inadequacies are:

1. Abnormally high or low pitch.
2. Lack of variation in pitch—vocal monotony.
3. Pitch patterns—rising or falling inflections regardless of meaning; identical inflections from phrase to phrase regardless of meaning.

Intensity—Inadequacies may include:

1. Abnormally loud or weak intensity.
2. Lack of variation in intensity; lack of emphasis.
3. Intensity patterns—the same variation in intensity regardless of meaning, for example, starting each sentence with more intensity than is used at its ending.

Duration—Among the possible inadequacies are:

1. Tones held for too short a time, resulting in a staccato effect.
2. Tones held for too long a time, resulting in an unpleasant drawl.
3. Lack of variability of rate of speech with all tones given about the same duration, resulting in vocal monotony and lack of emphasis.

Quality—Types of inadequacies (which were more fully discussed in Section 2) are as follows:

1. Muffled—too much resonance from the throat cavity.
2. Metallic—too much resonance from the mouth cavity.
3. Nasal—too much resonance from the nasal cavities.
4. Denasal—little or no resonance from the nasal passages.
5. Harsh—raucous, unpleasant.
6. Hoarse-husky—tense muscles in the mechanism, especially the throat, and possible unhealthy conditions in the cavities.
7. Breathy—the speaker's breath is heard above his vocal tones.
8. Infantile—has the characteristics of a young child's voice.

Flexibility—Lack of vocal flexibility is evidenced in monotony of pitch, intensity, duration, and quality in the speaker's expression of his meanings. The speaker seems to lack the ability to control these vocal attributes as he speaks. His vocal mechanism is not necessarily inflexible. He simply does not make it function at its best, if at all.

Improvement—If you are found to be inadequate in any of these items, you will want to attack your deficiency soon. Your instructor may help outline a program of retraining for you, which will include many of the following bases for the improvement of phonation.

Hear your own voice—You must learn to hear your voice as others hear it. You should know its good characteristics and hear them. You should know its bad characteristics and hear *them* when they occur. Your ear should tell you when your voice is functioning at its normal, natural best. A strong hearing sensitivity to the tones of your own voice is a first essential in voice improvement.

Your ear should hear in your own voice:

1. Its habitual pitch level.
2. Its normal natural pitch range from the highest pitched sounds you make to your lowest.
3. Its pitch inflections upward and downward.
4. Its loud tones and its weak tones.
5. Its short, staccato, jerky tones, and its tones which drawl noticeably.
6. The various kinds of bad voice quality, such as nasal, muffled, and so on.

Relaxed mechanism—Your entire speaking mechanism should be relaxed, so to speak, while you are speaking. It should be free from abnormal muscle tenseness or tightness. A relaxed mechanism is the result of:

1. Good health, both physical and mental.
2. A proper understanding of what is expected of you when you speak, as we noted in considering adjustment to the speaking situation.
3. Confidence, through familiarity with your general subject and thorough preparation of the speech to be given.
4. Absence of stage fright and uncertainty, through experience in meeting speaking situations. The result of experience is a comfortable poise and a natural control of the functioning of the bodily mechanism during speech.

Optimum pitch and pitch range—As you speak, the pitch of your voice fluctuates over a range of different pitches from low to high and high to low. Somewhere between the highest and lowest pitch your voice is capable of producing, there is a pitch level that is most natural for you. The pitch fluctuations of your voice seem to go up and down from this basic pitch level. You use it normally when you are relaxed, at ease, and not emotionally disturbed.

It is clear that the basic pitch level of men's voices is markedly lower than that of women. The average pitch level of male voices is approximately 128 vibrations per second. The pitch level of female voices is approximately 256 vibrations per second, or about Middle C on the musical scale.

Some male voices are naturally lower or higher in pitch than others. The same phenomenon is true of female voices. Since there is a basic pitch level best for each individual, you must discover and make a habit of using that basic pitch level which is natural and best for you. In addition, you should discover your natural pitch range from lowest to highest and make the use of it habitual.

Many speakers, particularly among women, tend to use a higher pitch level than is natural for them. They tend also to use more high than low pitches in their pitch range, which usually is not natural for them either. The rule therefore is: speak at your natural pitch level and use your normal pitch range. *Your basic pitch level should be medium or low for you.* You should avoid too much use of the higher levels of your pitch range. Do not, however, try to lower your pitch level by refusing to use occasional high pitch variations. To force your pitch down and hold it there will result in a low monopitch, which is also unattractive.

Reserve of intensity—You should have a strong voice. It should have a reserve of intensity that is not easily exhausted. You should have no trouble in making your audience hear in the average auditorium. To have a strong voice, you must:

1. Have a strongly active breathing mechanism. The muscles of respiration must act, during speech, with energy and power.
2. Cause a series of strongly vibrating breath waves to come from your larynx. These produce the pitches you desire.
3. At the same time, adjust the cavities of your throat, mouth, and nose.
4. Hold the adjustment of the cavities constant and continue the strongly vibrating breath waves until the tone has been built up by the resonance cavities to its full intensity.

12 Articulation

Characteristics—Articulation refers to the modification of the vocal tones, systematically, to form the speech sounds in connected oral discourse. The speech sounds consist in general of vowels, consonants, and diphthongs.

A speaker is superior in articulation when the speech sounds are formed correctly, accurately, and fluently. Such a speech pattern is characterized by clear vowels and diphthongs and by precise articulation of the consonants, free from noticeable hesitations and interruptions. Precision, clarity, and beauty describe the speech pattern thus produced.

Articulation Inadequacies—In diagnosing the adequacy of the process of articulation, the skilled observer makes special note of the following:

Organic disorders—Abnormalities of teeth, tongue, lips, palates, and face muscles.

Disorders of rhythm—Stuttering; jerky, hesitant, uneven sound formation.

Disorders of sound formation—Incorrect formation of certain of the speech sounds; inaccurate formation of consonants; slovenly articulation resulting from carelessness, inactivity of the articulators, or a rapid rate of utterance; foreign accent or dialect.

Improvement—If you are found to be inadequate in any of these items, you will want to correct your deficiency soon. Your instructor will help outline a program of retraining for you. Note the points outlined below as a basis for this retraining program.

Flexibility—You should have a flexible, active mechanism capable of making multitudinous, rapid, skilled movements. It has already been indicated that the tongue, lips, and soft palate should be active and flexible. The lower jaw, particularly, should be active; it should be free from tension and loose.

Hearing—You should be conscious of and critical of the formation of your own speech sounds. You should be able to recognize deviations from the correct formation in the speech of others.

Correct speech sound formation—You should be able to form the consonants correctly. Consonants are vitally important to speech. They are largely responsible for its intelligibility and distinctness. A consonant is formed by a stoppage or interference with the outward-moving breath stream in a specific manner to create a specific sound. Consonants are either voiceless or voiced. The vocal cords do not vibrate in the production of a voiceless consonant; vibration of the vocal cords is essential in the production of a voiced consonant.

The consonants are listed below. Note the italicized letters. You may wish to learn the International Phonetic Alphabet symbol for each consonant as indicated.

	Voiced			*Voiceless*	
Symbol	*Word*	*Phonetic tran-scription*	*Symbol*	*Word*	*Phonetic tran-scription*
[b]	bit	[bɪt]	[p]	pit	[pɪt]
[d]	din	[dɪn]	[t]	tin	[tɪn]
[g]	get	[gɛt]	[k]	kit	[kɪt]
[z]	zoo	[zu]	[s]	sue	[su]
[v]	vim	[vɪm]	[f]	fat	[fæt]
[w]	wet	[wɛt]	[ʍ]	whet	[ʍɛt]
[ð]	then	[ðɛn]	[θ]	thin	[θɪn]
[ʒ]	garage	[gəraʒ]	[ʃ]	shed	[ʃɛd]
[dʒ]	judge	[dʒʌdʒ]	[tʃ]	cheap	[tʃip]
[m]	me	[mi]			
[n]	neat	[nit]			
[ŋ]	sing	[sɪŋ]			
[l]	lead	[lid]			
[r]	read	[rid]			
[h]	hid	[hɪd]			
[j]	yet	[jɛt]			

You should be able to form the vowel sounds correctly. Vowels give tonal quality or vocality to speech. A vowel is a voiced speech sound in which there is little interference with the outgoing air. Each different vowel, when properly formed, is the result of an integrated adjustment of the cavities of the mouth, throat, and nose and their openings. This adjustment must be sustained momentarily for the intensity and richness of the sound to be built up. The most common vowel sounds used in general American speech are listed below.

Symbol	*Word*	*Phonetic tran-scription*	*Symbol*	*Word*	*Phonetic tran-scription*
[i]	eat	[it]	[u]	boom	[bum]
[ɪ]	it	[ɪt]	[ʊ]	book	[bʊk]
[e]	agent	[edʒənt]	[o]	omit	[omɪt]
[ɛ]	met	[mɛt]	[ɔ]	law	[lɔ]
[æ]	at	[æt]	[ɑ]	alms	[ɑmz]
[ə]	above	[əbʌv]	[ʌ]	buck	[bʌk]

You should use clear vowels. Allow time for the vowel to form and to secure the desired intensity and quality. Avoid muffling the vowel sounds by failure to open your mouth sufficiently to allow unimpeded emission of the modified breath stream.

The diphthong is made up of two vowels so closely blended that they lose their identity as individual sounds and become instead a new sound. The following diphthongs are used in general American speech. Check with your instructor as you make each sound, being sure that you understand the regional variations that you may have.

Symbol	Word	Phonetic transcription	Symbol	Word	Phonetic transcription
[eɪ]	maim	[meɪm]	[ou]	show	[ʃou]
[aɪ]	ice	[aɪs]	[au]	how	[hau]
[ɔɪ]	boy	[bɔɪ]	[ju]	mute	[mjut]

Accuracy—You should utter the sounds, as combined in words, with sufficient accuracy to insure adequate reception by the listener. Take time in forming the consonants in their relation to other sounds to allow for adequate formation. Use an equal distribution of breath; avoid the habit of using more breath force at the beginning than at the end of a word. You should, when required, be able to make a firm closure with an accompanying quick release of the blocked air. Avoid allowing too much breath to escape, which results in noisy or hissing sounds.

You should overcome lack of precision in articulation by avoiding certain common errors. For example, you should avoid talking too rapidly, more rapidly than the ease and accuracy of adjustment of your mechanism will allow. Avoid slurring—running sounds, syllables, or words together—[ʌəzæt] (what's that?), [dəwanə] (don't want to). Avoid weakening or eliminating final consonants such as [slɛp] (slept), [artɪs] (artists), [hæn] (hand), [faɪ] (five).

You should avoid lack of precision in articulating the middle consonants. Don't slur—[ən3ˑstæn] (understand), [gʌv3ˑmənt] (government), [ædʒətɪv] (adjective). Don't give tone to voiceless consonants—[wɔdɚ] (water), [ɪndəmədlɪ] (intimately), [bæbdɪst] (Baptist). Don't make voiced consonants voiceless—[bɪsnɪs] (business), [tris] (trees). You will notice the symbols [ɝ] and [ɚ] in the above. They are sometimes called "semivowels." They are formed by producing the sound of the vowel [ɜ] or [ə], and adding an [r] characteristic to each.

Fluency—As you speak, you should utter and combine the sounds fluently and rhythmically. Speech is not composed of separate sounds, but is an integration, in a necessary order and relationship, of sounds into syllables, syllables into words, and words into thought units. Repetition of, hesitations between, abnormally rapid or slow, or unusually precise or inaccurate utterance of sounds, syllables, and words makes for a jerky, uneven, discontinuous speech pattern, which may be difficult to understand and unpleasant to listen to. It is comforting to know that all speakers will have nonfluencies at times.

IV THE ESSENTIAL SKILLS
OF SPEECH MAKING

Introduction

Goals of Speech Making—Speech making is a specialized form of speaking in which one individual presents his thoughts or the thoughts of another on a given subject to a group of listeners for their benefit or for the benefit of himself or for the benefit of a cause. His immediate goal may be one or all of the following:

1. To inform or instruct.
2. To secure belief or action through persuasion.
3. To entertain or amuse.

Burdens of the Speaker—Regardless of his goal, the speaker must assume four fundamental burdens:

1. He must gain the attention of the audience and interest them in himself and his subject.
2. He must hold their attention and interest in spite of factors that may cause attention and interest to lag or fluctuate.
3. He must make his ideas clear to his audience in order that they may understand his thoughts exactly.
4. He must make them remember his thoughts and their relation to one another and to the central thought of his speech.

Essential Skills of Speech Making—To accomplish the above, skill in the essentials of speech making is required. These essentials are:

1. Choice of Subject
2. Choice of Thought
3. Choice of Material
4. Organization of Material
5. Use of Language
6. Projection to the Audience
7. Control of Bodily Activity
8. Rhythm
9. Pronunciation
10. Voice Control

Definitions of these essentials and principles involved follow.

13   *Choice of Subject*

Suited to the Audience—Select a general subject that is suited to the specific audience to which you will speak. Analyze your probable audience to determine their interests. Select the general subject only after you have ascertained all the facts you can about them and the situation. Remember, first of all, that your audience is composed of human beings. They must be interested if you wish them to attend to what you have to say. Remember also that you *can* interest them if you will.

In selecting your subject, ask yourself the following questions and be guided by the answers you make to them:

1. What will be the probable age range of my listeners?
2. Are my listeners likely to be intelligent, educated, and cultured— or otherwise?
3. What common interests are my listeners likely to have?
4. Will my audience be male, female, or mixed?
5. What are my listeners likely to know about me? Will they be likely to have confidence in me when speaking on the subject I choose?
6. Why will the audience to which I will speak have gathered? Will it have gathered to commemorate some special day or event, to decide upon a course of action, to be inspired, to be informed, or to be entertained?

7. What will my audience be likely to expect? What subject would it probably like to hear discussed?
8. What will be its probable mood, state of mind, attitude, and desires? Will it be boisterous, enthusiastic, docile, indifferent, anxious, or drowsy? Will it be prejudiced or free from prejudice?
9. What event or events have taken place recently that have gained general interest, approval, or disapproval?
10. What type of subject will my audience consider worthwhile listening to? (This question does not imply that it is necessary for you to speak on weighty topics. It simply is a warning that your audience will be pleased only if they feel that the time spent in listening to you has been time profitably spent.)

Suited to the Speaker—Select a general subject that is suited to you, the speaker. It *should come from a background with which you are intimately familiar.* You should be an authority on each subject you choose to speak upon. Never forget this principle.

Any subject you choose should be one in which you are vitally interested. You may have had experiences related to it. You may enjoy reading about it. You may enjoy discussing it or telling others about it.

Give the type of speech which your judgment and experience tell you you can give most successfully. Don't choose a subject unless you are reasonably sure you can make a success of it with the specific audience to which you will speak. Don't disappoint your audience by a poor choice of subject.

For mature speakers, facing speaking situations arising from their business, community, or family activities, choice of subject is usually not a problem. The immediate situation, the speaker's interests, his knowledge, his attitudes, his feelings, his desire to or the necessity for him to present his ideas will determine the subject upon which he speaks. But in your speech class, what subject to choose may seem to be quite a problem. However, you really do have quite a range of subjects to choose from, as indicated by the following list of possibilities:

1. Your subject may concern your vocation—your job or your studies.
2. It may concern your avocation—your hobbies in sports, science, nature, religion, art, collecting, writing, reading, or speaking.
3. It may be an explanation and description of an event, an invention, a law, a process, a philosophy, or a game. If you choose a subject of this type, your success will depend upon your ability to be clear as well as interesting.
4. It may be a presentation and discussion of an experience or a series of experiences which you have had.
5. It may be a discussion of something you have read. If you choose this type of subject, *discuss* what you have read, rather than merely reporting the content of a book, magazine article, or news story.

6. It may be a discussion of an individual, contemporary or historical, an evaluation of his life or an event in his life, an evaluation of his achievement.
7. It may be a belief that you hold or an opinion that you wish to support.
8. It may be the expression of a desire, a hope, a wish, or a prophecy, the discussion of which will stamp you as original, a leader of thought, and as a consequence give you great satisfaction.
9. If you are a humorist, if you are clever in the use of language, if you are skilled in the development of comic situations, if you can present the comic side of life *humorously* and with a point, do not hesitate to choose such a subject.

Do not make choice of subject for your class speaking assignments difficult. Almost anything within your experience will serve you well. Just be sure that it is sufficiently vivid and meaningful to make the speech easy to present to others with spontaneity, clarity, and interest.

14   *Choice of Thought*

Central Thought—Select from your general subject a specific phase of that subject, a central thought or main idea embodied in it, upon which you wish to dwell, that you wish your audience to consider in detail. The reasons for choosing a central thought are: to narrow the subject; to define its limits; to allow for concentration in order to give unity, coherence, and emphasis to the speech; and to make your goal or purpose clear to the audience.

Requirements of central thought—The central thought of your speech should meet the following requirements:

1. It should be an all-encompassing statement of the goal you wish to attain in your speech. It should be the main point upon which you wish your audience to focus their attention. It should be the main reason why you desire them to believe or do a certain thing.
2. All the thought and material to be included in your speech should be subordinate to it.
3. Its extent, the amount of thought and material it encompasses, should be proportionate to the time allotted to you by those requesting your appearance as a speaker. Ascertain this time limit before you prepare your speech. Your central thought should be sufficiently

limited and narrow to be completely developed within the time allowed. It should not be so broad that it cannot be completely developed within the time you are allowed.

Statement of central thought—The statement of the central thought should conform to the following:

1. It should contain one thought and one thought only.
2. It should be stated in the form of a complete sentence. It may be stated in declarative form, for example: "I want to outline for you the functioning of a football team in executing the triple-option play." It may be stated in the form of a question, for example: "What is a good procedure for tie-dyeing a shirt?"
3. It should be a specific statement. It should be short and simple, rather than long and involved. It should be instantly intelligible to, readily understood by, the audience. It should be easily remembered by the audience. It should stimulate and arouse the immediate interest of the audience.

Nature of Thought for Speeches—The thought process which you use in the development of your subject will depend upon what you expect to accomplish with your audience, as indicated by your central thought. Your thought pattern may be of three basic types:

1. To inform—The nature of your thought may be to give information, to make clear that which may not be clear to your audience. You may use any or all of the following devices: You may use *exposition,* in which you explain and amplify your thoughts, change the unfamiliar into the familiar, bring about understanding of terms, facts, things, points of view, beliefs, processes, or organizations. You may use *narration,* in which you recount experiences, events, and stories, real, fictional, or biographical. You may use *description,* in which you tell how that which is to be described affected your senses, how it looked, smelled, tasted, sounded, or felt.

2. To persuade—Your plan may be to follow the sequence of persuading, in which case you endeavor to influence your audience "to believe or act as you wish them to believe or act." You assume a burden of proof, you presume opposition, and you "state your case, then prove it." You must take a definite position for or against a proposition. You must not straddle the issue; you cannot favor both sides. You must appeal to the reason, the intelligence of your audience. You must choose and present arguments that are very valuable in proving the soundness and expediency of your central thought. You must also appeal to the feelings, the emotions, wants, likes, and dislikes of your audience if you expect to be persuasive. By relating your appeal both to the reason of your audience and to their feelings and emotions, you are more certain to gain the desired result. Any appeal to reason that is not also an appeal to a want is seldom effective. Some of the common feelings and wants are love, fear, hate, patriotism, devotion, pity, sympathy, cleanliness, morality, comfort, security, ownership, efficiency, social esteem, pride, honor, right, duty, and power.

3. To entertain—The nature of your thought may be to amuse, to entertain, to thrill, or to while away the time of the audience in a pleasant, stimulating manner. What you present must actually amuse, entertain, or thrill. The central thought of this type of speech is your immediate goal: the amusement and entertainment of your audience. The thought process used in the development of such a central thought are the stories, incidents, and circumstances you relate.

Subordinate Points—Analyze your central thought. Break it up into its elements, its component parts, and its subordinate points. Group your knowledge relative to your central thought into natural and inherent, not artificial, units. Each unit should be a subdivision of the central thought, a subsidiary idea or thought, a subordinate point. Be guided by the following suggestions: there must be more than one subdivision, or point; each point should develop the central thought directly; each point should include a single thought; there must be no overlapping; the points taken together should completely develop the central thought.

Audience analysis—Analyze your audience in terms of your central thought. Estimate their probable knowledge relative to it and their probable capacity for comprehension of it. Consider their probable interest in it and their prejudices toward it.

Selection of subordinate points—Evaluate the subordinate points of your central thought for the purpose of selecting those which must be presented to your audience. The points you wish to present may vary with the composition of your audience. Select those points which are essential to the development of the basic aspects of your central thought, which are necessary to insure comprehension by your audience, and which are likely to be of most interest to the audience. Eliminate all points which are not vital to the complete development of your central thought and which are not essential in securing the interest or comprehension of your audience. Avoid using too many points. The audience can remember and absorb five or six, but not many more. The use of too many points is usually the result of poor analysis of your central thought or the choice of one that is too broad.

Statement of subordinate points—Formulate each subordinate point in a stimulating, concise, and specific statement. Each point should be stated in the form of a complete sentence. Each point should be stated clearly and specifically, not generally. Each should be simple, easily understood, and easily remembered. Each should be stated so that it may be readily distinguished from each other point. At times, statement of points in parallel form is a good thing.

15   Choice of Material

Develop Subordinate Points—The central thought and its subordinate points must be developed, amplified, enlarged upon, and emphasized in order to insure interest, understanding, and belief on the part of the audience. The types of material to be used are dependent upon the nature of the central thought and its subordinate points and the audience to which the speech is to be presented. The types of material listed below should be used as indicated when necessary:

Explanation—The development and emphasis of your thought may be accomplished by explaining or translating for your audience the meaning and significance of your ideas or by simplifying, explaining, interpreting, or restating. You simply talk *about* your idea. For example, you may clarify your thought or unfold its meaning by restating it in simpler words or forms. You may outline or list the characteristics of your thought, its essential aspects, thus distinguishing it from others and making its meaning and significance clear. You may split your thought into its parts or elements in order to simplify it and make it clear. Or you may make your thought clear by commenting upon the derivation or the source of unfamiliar words or terms.

Specific instances—The development and emphasis of your thought may be accomplished by relating specific instances or circumstances within your experience and the experience of the audience which illustrate the points you wish to make clear. Be certain that each instance or circumstance has a point, the point in question, and be certain that you make that point clear. For example, you may relate one or more personal experiences. Or you may tell a story or a series of stories, humorous or serious, which you have read or heard. Or you may set up hypothetical situations based on truth or fiction.

In relating experiences, stories, events, or hypothetical situations, select carefully the details to be presented. Use only those details which are essential to the development of the point involved in each story, instance, or circumstance and which are necessary to give it its proper setting, color, and flavor.

Comparison and contrast—The development and emphasis of your thought may be accomplished by use of comparison and contrast. You may compare and contrast ideas, objects, mechanical devices, principles, policies, theories, philosophies, persons, and so on. For example, you may make your point clear by indicating its similarity or likeness to something familiar or known to the audience. Or you may make your point clear by indicating its dissimilarity or unlikeness in the same way. Choose that material which is best suited to simple, natural, direct, exact, and fair comparison or contrast and which is especially helpful in making your point. Avoid complicated and remote comparisons.

Statistics—The development of your thought may be accomplished by the use of statistics. In establishing your point, use statistics that are incontrovertible and authoritative. They must not be based on rumor or hearsay. Use statistics your audience can comprehend. The mere use of figures does not guarantee comprehension or belief. If your statistics are difficult for the audience to visualize or comprehend, incorporate them in examples or accompany them with simple, familiar illustrations. Be exact in your statement of the statistics you present. Put them on a note card and read them verbatim if necessary. Usually, it is best to quote your statistics in round numbers. For example, quote $1,592,871.61 as $1,593,-000 or $1,600,000, depending upon the need for exactness. It is wise to state the source of your statistics: the authority, the name of the publication, the publisher, the date of publication, and the page reference.

Interpret the meaning of your statistics as they relate to the point you wish to make. Apply them to the point. Make them meaningful. Your audience may not remember the statistics you quote, but they should remember the point they develop.

Opinion—The development of your thought may be accomplished by the use of opinions, interpretations, conclusions, and beliefs of yourself and others. Opinions are not facts and they are not necessarily true statements. Their value depends upon the competence and reputation of the person who makes them. You may state your own opinions if they are the result of careful thought and not merely hasty generalization. You should be able to give reasons and supporting evidence for your opinion if necessary. You may state the opinion of a friend if he is competent to express an opinion on the point in question. Or you may state the opinion of an authority or several authorities on the point in question. In this case, be sure the authority is especially competent, a thorough student of the subject upon which he is quoted. He should be a well-known man of good reputation for his testimony to be readily acceptable to the audience. If he is not well known but is competent, it may be necessary to establish him as competent. He must be unbiased for his opinion to be reliable and valid. If you quote the opinions of authorities, quote them exactly. It is better to read the quotations verbatim from a note card. State in full the source of the opinion quoted.

Interpret the significance of your opinions and the statements from authority which you quote as they relate to the point you wish to make. Apply them to the point; make them meaningful.

Amount of Material—Choose material that will develop each subordinate point fully, adequately, and completely. Do not choose more material than the development of each point demands. The amount necessary should be determined by the nature of the point and the specific audience to which you speak. Do not use more details than you can reasonably expect your audience to assimilate and comprehend in the time allowed. Your audience may become confused if you use too many details, facts, or illustrations. If you use too much material, you may not have time to relate it properly to the point and to the central thought of your speech or to adapt it adequately to your audience. A multitude of details may obscure your point.

Do not rely on an insufficient amount of material in the development of your points. You cannot expect to be clear and effective nor to accomplish your objective if your material is too limited. If your points are not fully developed, or if your ideas lack support and substantiation, your speech is likely to be all talk—"hot air," as is sometimes said. Your audience will accuse you of having nothing to say, of not knowing your subject, and will become bored and not listen. Your speech will be trite, ordinary, uninteresting, and inconsequential. With too little material you may be guilty of hasty generalization.

If you need material—If you need more material for developing your points, you must change the central thought of your speech or find the needed material. To change the central thought of your speech is often the most advisable thing to do in such a case. If the subject had developed out of a background with which you were familiar, you would not be faced with the necessity of finding more material. You should never choose a subject for a speech unless material for its development is readily available.

Or try to accumulate concrete, specific material to develop your central thought if you feel that you need it. However, avoid the common error of using but one source for all of your material. Recall related experiences that you have had and select those that may be useful in developing your points. Discuss your subject with friends for purposes of gathering illustrations and opinions. Consult recognized authorities, in person, for source material or specific information and examples. Examine the current newspapers and magazines for recent information, examples, statistics, and opinions. Visit the library. Consult the librarian. Look in general reference books, encyclopedias, *The World Almanac,* and others. Consult the *New York Times Index* and *The Reader's Guide* for references to comparatively recent materials in the newspapers and magazines. Also, use the library card index to locate books related to your subject.

Relevant, reliable, consistent, convincing material—Choose relevant, reliab'e, consistent, and convincing material for the development of your points. Also, be sure to interpret accurately the material you choose. Do not let prejudices, likes, and dislikes influence you in the choice or interpretation of your material. Choose only relevant material—material directly related to your point. Beware of using unrelated material. Keep to the point—don't wander from it. Choose only the most reliable material—

material that the audience will accept without question. Is it hearsay, rumor, or gossip? Does it come from reliable sources? Is it ethical for you to ask your listeners to accept it? It is folly to choose and present questionable material in the development of your points. Choose only material which is consistent and compatible. For example, it must be in accord with (not inconsistent with) and logically develop the point in question. It must be in agreement with and not contradict materials used elsewhere in your speech. If presented as factual, it must not be inconsistent with fact or reality. Each separate bit of material must be logically consistent and coherent.

Suited to your audience—Choose material in the development of your points that is suited to your probable audience. Choose your material only after a careful analysis of that probable audience, as follows:

1. For interest—Choose material that will create the greatest possible interest on the part of your audience, so that it will catch their attention immediately. Choose material closely related to the experience of your audience. Choose material that is related to human motives and desires such as money, power, reputation, happiness, honor, right, or duty. Remember that your audience is composed of human beings. Human beings are, basically, much the same. You will fail if you talk over the heads of your audience by using abstract and impersonal material.

Choose material that has inherent attention values, which by its very nature gets attention. Use novel and striking rather than ordinary, commonplace, inconsequential materials. Choose material that will arouse the curiosity of your audience. An audience that is curious will not be difficult to keep interested. Choose material that will aid you in creating in your audience a feeling of suspense. Develop in them a state of mental apprehension and anxiety about what you have to say. The suspense factor, when properly used, is a great asset to a speaker. Choose material which has an aspect of the sensational. Here you may use startling but well-founded material. You are warned, however, to be reasonable. Don't be an alarmist.

Whenever possible, choose humorous material to accompany the more weighty and serious material. If your subject lends itself to the introduction of humor, avail yourself of the opportunity. Don't be too serious. Remember that "A bit of nonsense, now and then, is relished by the wisest men." A wise selection of humor makes for a pleasant response on the part of the audience. It may reduce undesirable tensions, provide relaxation, and increase the friendliness, interest, and attention of the audience. But be sure that the humor is suited to your subject and audience and is applicable to the point you are making.

2. For clarity—Choose material for the development of your points that will aid you in being clear. You will fail if you allow your audience to become hazy, perplexed, or uncertain as to what you mean. What you have in mind should always be self-evident from the material you use. Be clear, through wise choice of material. Choose vivid, colorful material. Picture your thoughts plainly. Generally, for most audiences, it is wise to use illustrations, examples, comparisons, and contrasts freely. Create vivid images and set them out in bold relief; use brilliant, broad, bold strokes. More often than not, most of your speech should consist of illustrative material, the most important factor in being clear.

Choose simple rather than complicated material. It is better to be easy to understand than hard to understand. In the latter case, you are more often likely to be misunderstood. Choose only that material which is within the range of the experience and the imagination of your audience. Don't talk "over the heads" of your audience by using material which is far removed from everyday life. When possible, choose illustrative material which has aspects of the familiar. Secure understanding from the audience by proceeding from things that they know about to the new ideas you want them to have. Lead them into an understanding and appreciation of the new through relating it to the old.

Assimilate, Adapt, Interpret Your Material—Make your speech a worthwhile representation of your own work. Your contribution to your audience is based upon what you do with your material after you have chosen it. Study your material, digest it, and assimilate it. Rework it so that it represents a real part of your own knowledge. Think about its application to your subject and your audience. Your job is only partly done when you have chosen your material.

Adapt your material to your central thought, points, and audience. Relate it to the central thought and to the points which you use. Actually use your material to develop your central thought. Do not let the audience supply relationships. Too many speakers simply report facts, statistics, or opinions without interpreting their meaning. A report of an event, a trip, or the content of a news story or magazine article is not a speech as properly conceived. Do not be merely a reporter, a statistician, a walking encyclopedia. Do not give the audience the idea that you have nothing to offer but a dry statement and classification of facts. You will fail if you do not interpret, evaluate, apply, and structuralize your material in a way that makes it have extraordinary significance for the immediate audience.

Visual Aids for Presenting Material—Some material can be presented most effectively, quickly, and understandably if a visual aid is used. There are many kinds of visual aids. Each has values and disadvantages.

The blackboard—You will find a blackboard in nearly every classroom. It can be used upon impulse. It is interesting for the audience to watch as the speaker writes. There is no expense involved and there are no bothersome materials to be carried around.

The disadvantages come from a lack of planning. Speakers may become absorbed in their writing and keep looking at the board. Their bodies may hide the material as they write. They may become too involved in the appearance of the drawing itself and keep erasing and redrawing. Speakers may distract the attention of the audience by apologizing for the poor artistic work. They may take too long to put things on the board. The drawings must be erased when the speaker is through, and then they are gone for good.

Easel pads—These have some of the advantages of the blackboard. They may be worked on in the presence of the audience. They can be partially prepared in advance with light pencil lines, which are followed with a marker during presentation. They can be kept and used over again. The expense is nominal. The use of color is an added possibility.

The disadvantages are that the pads call for a particular kind of easel and that they are awkward for an inexperienced speaker to work with.

Objects—If your can show something as you talk about it, you can save a thousand descriptive words.

But you will have problems. Sometimes the object cannot be seen especially if it has an "inside" which is important in the speech, such as some device whose operation is being described.

You should not pass an object around, because it distracts attention from the speaker.

Blown-up pictures—They are dramatic visual aids. Even small pictures can be useful. Mount them in groups on a large cardboard. Display the board. Walk toward the audience with it, holding it out. But, again, don't pass it around. Suggest that if the listeners wish to see the pictures in greater detail, they will be able to do so after the speech. Point out to them what they are looking at as you hold the display.

Charts and graphs—These may be the very best visual aids. They can be carefully planned in advance. They can be selective, in that only the material you choose to present is displayed. You can show relationships by the use of color and space. Comparisons are possible. Charts and graphs are easily handled, quickly removed, and available for exhibiting again and again.

The problem comes in the preparation. These aids take time to plan and execute. Will the effort be worth the value to the speech? This is something you cannot measure precisely. You just decide.

Handouts—They have some very valuable characteristics. They can be in the hands of everyone at the same time. They can include a considerable amount of printing—something you should not try to put on the board, something that would make a chart or graph too cluttered. A series of dates and events, for example, is more appropriate in a handout.

There is always the problem of duplication. Mimeograph and ditto serve well for distribution to large audiences. If the number of listeners is small, say up to twenty, it is possible to use a mechanical-photo process which reproduces the printing on the original page, just as it looked, including pictures. But the cost factor will have to be considered.

Visual aids take time and effort, but they are worth it.

16   Organization of Material

You must organize your thought and material *for* your probable audience. You must structure it so that they can visualize it as a whole, always seeing its parts as they relate to the whole. You will thus implant in the minds of your audience your central thought, its subordinate points, and the material used in their development. If you organize your thought and material well, your audience will follow your presentation easily and without effort. You will be readily understood, and your thought will be easily remembered. Time spent in organizing thought and material is well worthwhile. An outline is of great value in the organization process. Before continuing with an organization formula, let us examine some of the paperwork involved in speech making.

Manuscripts, Outlines, and Speaker's Notes—Only the impromptu speech is made without any aids in preparation and presentation, and even the impromptu speaker may use a scribbled note or two if he has a few minutes to think before he makes his talk. Any old envelope will do. Just put down a few words to keep you on the track. They may be out of order as you think of them, so you may need to put some arrows or asterisks or numbers on the notes to put them into proper order for your speech.

Order—that is the key word. The main reason for developing an outline is to arrange your thoughts in order. Order is the arrangement of phone numbers by groups in the yellow pages. It is the arrangement of items by groups in the classified section of the newspaper. It is the arrangement of material by groups in your filing cabinet.

The outline—An outline is invaluable. Develop it in preparation. Avoid it in presentation.

Do not take it to the speaker's stand when you speak. Take a manuscript or speaker's notes (more on that later).

Start on your outline as soon as you have selected your topic.

The first step is to begin grouping your ideas, and to do that you need "groupers," a set of symbols that point out relationships. Use letters and numbers, alternately. Here is the usual order, with subordination indicated by indentation:

I.
  A.
    1.
      a.
      b.
    2.
  B.
II.

Remember that you must have at least two items in each group. In other words, if you have "A," you must have "B."

Begin with the following four parts of a speech and use Roman numerals for them:

I. Introduction

II. Central Thought

III. Body

IV. Conclusion

Use capital letters for the main points or divisions in each part. Divide the main points into subordinate points with Arabic numerals. In case you want to include details, use lower-case letters. Some speakers subdivide further, using numerals and letters in parentheses, and even brackets, but that is probably further than you will go for most speeches you will ever make.

Develop the body first. As you begin your work you select a topic, decide on your general purpose, and formulate a central thought. At some time you will want to jot down as many ideas as you can about your topic. Do it quickly. Don't evaluate each idea as you put it down. Leave that for later. Just get the ideas down. Then group them under the main headings indicated by the capital letters and indented.

Be sure to indent. This gives a pictorial impression of subordinate relationships.

Then add the details. Finally, develop the conclusion and the introduction. You may even want to write out the first sentence or two of the introduction, so that you will know *exactly* what you want to say when you begin speaking. Don't leave it completely to the chairman's introduction and your response to him. Plan your opening as you make your outline.

Write out the last couple of sentences of the conclusion as well. They will help you terminate your speech in confidence. You will not just run out of things to say, finally mumbling "Thank you," and going to sit down. Say "Thank you" if you want to, but do it as though you intended to do it. Plan to say it.

Here is a sample of an outline for a speech. The subject is "Civil

Technology," the general purpose is to inform, and the title is "Working Out of Doors." Put these items at the end of the outline, so that you are not tempted to include them at the opening of your talk. Remember, you do not have to announce your title. The chairman will do that. If he forgets, it doesn't make much difference. A title is for purposes of identifying. When you begin to speak, it is too late to identify. You had better know what you came to say.

I. Introduction.
   A. Attention-getting materials.
      1. When I was twelve years old, my father taught me to drive a tractor and to plow a field. The best part of it was that the work was out of doors.
      2. I always liked being out of doors, working, playing, fishing, or riding.
   B. Leading into topic.
      1. I often thought about being someone who had a job outdoors, like a pilot, a fireman, or a carpenter.
      2. I found the perfect profession for me: civil technology.

II. Central Thought: I want to tell you about my field—what it is, how to become trained for it, and what the future holds.

II. Body.
   A. What is civil technology?
      1. Civil engineering is an old profession.
      2. Civil engineering technology is very new.
         a. Implies a craft to the major profession.
         b. Definition.
      3. There are two divisions in civil technology.
         a. Drafting.
         b. Construction.
            (1) National dollar volume.
            (2) Tops in number of people employed.
            (3) All phases of construction: surveyors, draftsmen, laboratory technicians, highway foremen.
   B. Where can you get training?
      1. Most states will have a program in one of their schools of technology.
      2. The University of Houston has a fine program.
         a. The overall program is comparable in general requirements to an engineering degree.
         b. Specific courses center around drafting, surveying, and materials.
   C. My experience has helped and my hopes for the future are high.
      1. Part-time jobs at home in construction.

    2. My work on construction while I am in school.

    3. I hope to have my own building company someday.

IV. Conclusion.

    A. Summary.

    B. Close: When I was a kid I was learning to work with equipment. It led to my field, which is civil technology. I am now here receiving on-the-job and in-school training. Someday, if you want someone to build you a building, come to me. You will probably find me on a job site somewhere, because I like working out of doors.

Topic: My Field—Civil Technology.

Purpose: To inform my audience about my field.

Title: Working Out of Doors.

Now that you have your outline, what will you do with it? Rehearse with it. Prepare a manuscript or speaker's notes from it, but be wary of taking it to the speaker's platform. You may have too much written down and you will try to read it. Or you may say some of the words that are only organizational symbols, such as "The title of my speech is working out of doors" or "My topic is civil technology."

The manuscript—If you are giving a speech that calls for a manuscript there are a number of steps to be taken. And please note, you do not begin by "writing a speech" in the same way you would write an essay.

First, prepare an outline as described above and rehearse the speech from the outline, saying it out loud. This way you will establish an "oral" quality to the words you say. You will include personal pronouns. There may be incomplete sentences—groups of words, punctuated with periods as though they were complete sentences. There will be contractions, such as *can't* and *don't*.

Try to write out what you said as you rehearsed. Then revise it into a reading copy, the one you will take to the platform. It should be typed or lettered unless you write with great legibility. Double-space the type. Skip lines if you are lettering or writing the speech by hand.

Leave wide margins. Let there be no carry-over sentences. It is best if each page begins with a new paragraph.

Then rehearse with the manuscript. Learn to look down and get two or three entire lines at a glance. Look at the audience as you say the words. Don't hurry. Keep a finger on the place if you want to, so that you will know where to look. Slide the papers to the side as you read. Don't lift up the top sheets and put the finished page under the pile. Don't bother to turn them over. Have them side by side, with two pages visible at a time. Be reading from one. As you near the bottom of the page, slide it to the side, so that the next page is visible before you need it.

Speaker's notes—If you are not using a manuscript, if you can resist the temptation to take your outline to the speaker's stand with you, but if you think you must have *something* with you at the podium, try speaker's notes.

Take a 4-by-6 card. Look at your outline. Select the key word from each item of the outline and put it on the card. Indent as the outline was indented to show relationships, so that you may use appropriate transitions as you go along.

Rehearse with the card. Put the card on the speaker's stand and leave it there. Don't play with it. If you come around the stand, hold the card easily in your hand.

If you need more than one card, try not to have more than four or five. You tend to play with them and they may get out of order. Write on only one side and have the cards plainly numbered.

You may choose to write your speaker's notes on a full sheet of paper. Try not to put much more on it than you do on a card. Otherwise it gets to look like an outline and you try to read it, thereby losing eye contact.

Underline eight or ten words to make the flow of the speech visibly clear.

Do not use more than two sheets. Lay them down on the speaker's stand and leave them alone. Try not to play with them. The whole reason for using outlines, manuscripts, and speaker's notes is to keep order in what you say and to make what you say clear and direct to the audience.

Organization Formula—The organization of your speech may be accomplished best by establishing four parts, each having a distinct function. These four parts are *Introduction, Central Thought, Body,* and *Conclusion.* The parts may vary in length and importance with the type of subject and the type of audience, but the four functions remain the same for all speaking situations.

1. The introduction—Your introduction should lead your audience up to a consideration of the central thought of your speech. It should "dispose" the audience favorably toward you. It should establish a common ground between you and your audience. It should establish in your audience a receptive attitude toward the central thought under consideration. You should *arouse* the attention and *stimulate* the interest of your audience.

In addition to the above, you may need, depending upon your central thought and your audience, to accomplish special functions in your introduction. It may be necessary for you to establish your right to address your audience on the subject chosen. In some cases you may need to give a history of your subject, to define unfamiliar terms, and to consider other necessary items. It may be necessary for you to remove prejudices, allay suspicion, and promote open-mindedness.

Length of introduction—The length of your introduction will vary with your central thought and your audience. If your audience is unfamiliar

with or prejudiced toward you or your subject or both, more time undoubtedly must be spent in your introduction than if the situation were otherwise
In general, a long speech requires a longer introduction than does a short
speech. As someone has said, "The introduction should be short enough
to be interesting and long enough to cover the subject." Some introductions have been no longer than one sentence.

Type of introduction—The type of introduction to use depends upon
your central thought and your audience. In any case, select that type of
introduction which is most appropriate. It may consist of one or several of
the following approaches: (1) You may make remarks concerning yourself
or refer to some experience of yours. (2) You may refer to the occasion,
the audience, or the reason for the meeting. (3) You may refer to the
subject, its timeliness, or its importance. (4) You may build up a dramatic
situation as a means of establishing a background for the development of
your central thought. (5) You may embody your introductory thoughts in
suitable illustrations. (6) You may tell a story or a series of stories
humorous or serious, which embody your introductory thought and establish a background for the development of your central thought. Do not
"drag in" funny stories for the sole purpose of making the audience laugh
Be sure that each story you use is appropriate to the subject and audience
and that each story has a point. Be sure that you clearly relate the point
of your story to what you are trying to accomplish in your introduction.

In preparing your introduction beware of giving the audience credit
for knowing either more or less about your subject than it does. Beware
of telling stories not bearing upon the subject; of leading the audience to
expect considerations not forthcoming, thereby giving them a false idea
of your goal; of dampening interest and destroying confidence by making
apologies; and of using an introduction which is too long.

2. Central thought—(See "Central Thought" under "Choice of
Thought," Section 14.) You should state your central thought at the end
of the introduction and before you begin the body of the speech in which
its subordinate points are to be developed. You should state your central
thought at least three times during the course of the speech. You may
repeat it verbatim, state it in other words or another form, or amplify and
enlarge upon it simply and briefly. Be certain that your audience knows
exactly what you are talking about.

On the other hand, some experienced speakers, when they face a
peculiar speaking situation, may find it advisable to omit the statement of
the central thought altogether. Before an uncertain or hostile audience
it may be advisable to withhold for a time the statement of the central
thought. If the speaker elects to omit an explicit statement, the speech
must be so well developed that the central thought is established by im
plication. Omission of the central thought statement does not mean that
the speaker has no central thought—only that the statement is omitted
Inexperienced speakers should beware of omitting the statement of the
central thought.

3. The body—The function of the body of the speech is the development of your central thought in such a way that it interests your audience, is clearly and emphatically presented, and as a consequence is generally understood and remembered by them. The central thought should be developed as a unit. Subordinate points and materials should stand out only as they relate to the development of the central thought. The importance and the necessity of the following suggestions will vary with the intelligence of the audience, its knowledge of your central thought, and hence its ability to follow and absorb your thought and material.

All points should be subordinate to the central thought and presented so that the audience is aware of how each develops it directly. As you develop each point, state what it accomplishes and how it is related to the central thought. Incorrect inferences and relationships by your audience are thus prevented. Repeat each point and its relation to the central thought as you proceed to the following point. The audience is thus less likely to forget your points. Use transitions, relating the point completed to the point following. Your audience is thus certain to be carried from one thought to another without misunderstanding.

Development of subordinate points—Each subordinate point should be developed as a unit. Materials used in the development of a point should stand out only as they relate to the development of that point and the central point. All materials should be subordinated to the point in process of development and presented in such a way that the audience is aware of how each bit of material develops that point directly. As you present each bit of material, state what it accomplishes in the development of that point. Avoid using disconnected but related materials from which the audience must infer relationships. You should supply the necessary connection. If you do not, the audience may make the wrong inference or make none at all. As you complete the development of each point, briefly review and summarize the materials presented and state their application to the point in question.

Your materials should be handled so that the important details and the important relationships are remembered by the audience. For example, you should repeat the names of persons, places, things, dates, statistics, statements of authorities, complicated formulae, mechanical processes, or specific directions, if you wish them to be remembered. You should repeat a statement if its meaning is dependent upon a single word or a single syllable of a word. Repeat several times in the same or different words any detail or statement you wish to emphasize or which you wish your audience to remember. If you are not sure that you have made yourself clear or that the audience has assimilated the details of your material, do not hesitate to repeat and restate until you are certain that the audience visualizes and understands.

Arrangement of subordinate points—You should arrange your subordinate points, depending upon the central thought and the immediate audience, in an order best suited to insure the greatest understanding and the least confusion. Plan the best arrangement in advance, even though conditions in the audience may make it necessary to change the order of arrangement of your points at a moment's notice, before or after you have begun speaking. Always arrange your points systematically in terms of the goal, as defined by your central thought, which you wish to accomplish with your specific audience. Avoid a random, wandering, unsystematic arrangement of points.

It may be wise to arrange your points logically, having each succeeding point built upon and dependent upon the development of the former. In the development of a central thought which entails a great deal of exposition and description, this arrangement may be best. It may be necessary in persuasive and argumentative speaking with some thoughts and with some audiences.

It may be wise to arrange your points chronologically, having events follow a time order. Chronological order of arrangement is mandatory in the development of a central thought which must be treated in a historical manner.

It may be wise to arrange your points in climactic order, in which the most important, strongest, and most stimulating point occurs last. In narration, climactic order may be not only wise but necessary. In persuasive and argumentative speaking, the composition of the audience and the mental state of its members will be the determining factors in the use of climactic order of arrangement. With some audiences it may be wise to present the strongest and most important point first.

Arrangement of material for subordinate points—You should arrange the material to be used in the development of each subordinate point in the order best suited to the development of that point in terms of the audience to which you are speaking. What has been said above regarding the arrangement of the subordinate points can also be applied to the arrangement of the material in the development of each point. The following form is advisable in most cases, depending upon the amount and kind of material at your disposal. It is especially recommended for developing the points in persuasive speaking.

1. A statement of the point to be made.
2. A restatement of the point in another and perhaps simpler form to insure comprehension and emphasis.
3. Introductory material, necessary explanation and definition of terms.
4. General illustrations.
5. More specific illustrations.
6. Statements from authority.
7. Summary, restatement, application, and transition, in which you emphasize the point completed by reviewing its development, relating and connecting it to the thesis and that which follows.

4. The conclusion—Your conclusion should effectively and forcefully leave the central thought of your speech with your audience. It should restate and enforce the most important elements of your speech and relate them to your central thought, integrating the central thought with the motives and interests of your audience.

The type or kind of conclusion you use will vary with your central thought and immediate audience. Your conclusion may exercise one or all of the following functions: It may dispose your audience favorably toward you and your central thought; remarks of a personal nature are often used in this type of conclusion. It may amplify the merits of your central thought; additional exposition and illustrative material are often used. It may arouse your audience to heights of emotion, feeling, or deep concern by exhorting and exciting them to action. Or it may simply recapitulate or summarize the important points used in the development of your central thought.

In preparing your conclusion you should beware of taking more time than necessary to conclude; of introducing new ideas or points; of trying to "make amends" for an inadequate development of your central thought; of concluding by referring to the last point of your speech only; of leaving your speech unended and your audience uncertain; of failing to unify your speech by diffusing attention, rather than focusing it on your central thought and its subpoints; and of being anticlimactic, letting your audience down suddenly.

17 Use of Language

Thought Units and Sentences—Language is the basic factor in communication. To be communicative is to be understood. The degree to which the audience understands your thought is dependent, initially, upon the words you use and their arrangement into thought units. The thoughts of a speaker become clear as they are translated into words in meaningful combinations. Hence, adequacy in the use of language is based upon the arrangement of words in sentences.

You should construct your sentences carefully so that each idea is received by your audience as you intend it to be received. Construct your sentences so as to give your audience the complete and exact idea in an emphatic way. Use periodic sentences in which the important idea comes at the end. They provide opportunities for vocal emphasis and create suspense. Whenever it is possible, the words, phrases, or clauses that make up your sentence should be arranged climactically. When you can, use balanced sentences, in which similar or opposite ideas are "set off" against one another. Secure emphasis by separating an especially important idea from others and placing it in a sentence by itself. Do not place an important idea in a subordinate clause.

Vary the construction of your sentences by using declarative, imperative, and interrogative sentences. Use the rhetorical question, in which the answer is implied, with your audience supplying it mentally, if not actually. Use the direct question, the answer to which must be introduced by you.

Use variety in the length and complexity of your sentences. Use short sentences more frequently than long ones. Too many consecutive short sentences, however, make for a broken, choppy effect. Use simply constructed sentences more frequently than compound or complex ones. Too many simple sentences, however, may be offensive to some types of audiences.

You should use acceptable grammar in the formation of your sentences. Acceptable grammar is that used by the majority of educated people. You should try to avoid certain errors of sentence structure, such as incomplete sentences (fragments); stringy sentences (sentences which need to be broken up into smaller units); choppy sentences (short sentences which need to be combined). You should avoid excessive coordination of sentences. Do not string thought units together with "and," "for," "because," "but." Eliminate these connectives. You should avoid long and involved sentences.

You should also avoid unusual sequence, order, and arrangement in sentence structure. You should avoid using verbs which do not agree with the subject—"They was (were) going home." Avoid using the incorrect verb form in relation to the tense (past, present, future)—"The mail has came" (come). Avoid using incorrect sequence of tenses—"I planned to have stopped" (to stop). Avoid using pronouns incorrectly—"It is him" (he). Avoid using incorrect contractions—"He don't" (doesn't). Avoid using adjectives for adverbs—"He did good (well) as an athlete." Avoid mixed constructions—"I am not going nowhere" (I am not going anywhere), "They are as following:" (They are as follows:).

Vocabulary—The more skillfully your words are selected the clearer the translation of your thought is likely to be. You should choose words for the expression of your ideas which are instantly intelligible to your audience to insure comprehension and prevent misunderstanding. Choose words with specific and exact meanings to insure correct and clear understanding by your listeners. Specific words stimulate the listener's imagination to a full realization of your meaning more quickly than general and abstract words do.

You should choose vivid, colorful words in stating your thought, which will instantly stimulate the imagination of your audience and help them to visualize your idea in complete detail. You should choose a variety of words. Avoid using the same word over and over again. Do not appear to have a limited and narrow vocabulary. You should feel free to use personal pronouns (I, you, we), thus placing yourself in a more personal, direct relationship with your audience.

You should avoid annoying your audience by your word choice. For example, you should avoid unfamiliar words. You should not use words and phrases that exaggerate your ideas in an unwarranted manner, such as "absolutely" or "beyond a shadow of a doubt." You should avoid using common, hackneyed, meaningless expressions—"that thing," "and everything else," "and something else," "and so forth," "what-you-may-call-it," "day in and day out," "wheels of time"—lest you be dull, trite, unclear, and possibly misunderstood. Consider well whether you will use obscenities, crude slang, or ill-bred colloquialisms in your language. You want audience approval. How easily do you think they would be offended? Be sure you know the meaning of the words you use. Keep a dictionary and a thesaurus close at hand for frequent reference. You should avoid using too many words and inserting needless words. Finally, you should avoid the omission of words necessary to the complete expression of your idea.

You might be more interested in developing your sensitivity toward better use of language. Here is an exercise which provides practice in the use of a thesaurus to choose more appropriate words. You will need a thesaurus and a dictionary.

WORD STUDY EXERCISE

Select one of the following words:

1. variance	11. harmonious	21. mislead	31. defense
2. augmentation	12. costume	22. misrepresent	32. evidence
3. incorporate	13. shape	23. small	33. security
4. uniformity	14. aperture	24. neglect	34. opposition
5. duration	15. motility	25. copy	35. complete
6. priority	16. vagabond	26. absurd	36. irrelevant
7. youth	17. spring	27. increase	37. curious
8. continually	18. impetus	28. conceal	38. destroy
9. indomitable	19. advance	29. pain	39. command
10. energetic	20. introduce	30. frequent	40. disrepute

Using your thesaurus, work out the following answers:

   Edition of thesaurus _____

   Word found on page ____, with the following identification as to part of speech, category, division, subgroup, etc.:

(**Note:** Take the word "curious," number 37 in your list. In the alphabetical listing of the 1962 edition it is found on page 781. "Inquisitive" is given as one meaning, an adjective, numbered 526.5. That entry is found on page 343. It falls in Class 6, "Intellect." The division is II, "State of Mind," and the section is A, "Mental Attitude." The alphabetically arranged editions will not provide these classifications.)

Three synonyms, maintaining (noun, verb, etc.) _____ as the part of speech, are:

_____   _____   _____

Meanings of the three synonyms, using _____ as the dictionary reference, are:

    1. _____
    2. _____
    3. _____

Two antonyms, maintaining the same part of speech, are:

_____   _____

Meanings of the two antonyms:

    1. _____
    2. _____

Write sentences of ten words or more using each of the three synonyms and two antonyms studied. Try to develop each sentence in such a way that it carries out the meaning of the word. Underline the word for quick recognition.

    1.

    2.

    3.

    4.

    5.

18 Projection to the Audience

The term *projection to the audience* refers to the process by which the speaker sends forth his thoughts and feelings to the listener. It involves the initiation by the speaker, through the use of his voice and bodily activity, of the sound and light waves which carry his meanings to that listener. Effectiveness in projection is dependent upon the degree with which these sound and light waves vibrate with the full meaning and vigor of the speaker's thought and feeling. To project well, your bodily mechanism must function as a dynamic whole.

Effective projection to the audience will influence the reaction of the audience individually and as a group to the speaker and the speech as a whole. For the response of the audience to be adequate, good will toward the speaker and general appreciation and understanding of his speech, its content, and purpose must be evidenced at its conclusion. The speech itself must be sufficiently stimulating to get attention quickly and hold that attention easily. The personal qualities of the speaker, as well as his thought and his manner of speaking, must have a pleasing effect on his listeners. The audience must be favorably disposed toward him.

Know Your Speech—Be thoroughly prepared! You should know your material, what it means, and what its implications are. If you do, you will speak with spontaneity and abandon. You will not be troubled with having to think of what to say next. You cannot be uncertain about the plan and content of your speech and project well.

Your Attitude Is Vital—You should have a wholesome, positive, dynamic attitude that can be characterized as follows:

1. You should be confident of yourself and of your success. This is not egotism.
2. You should appear interested in your subject, your audience, and the task before you. Audiences like the confident, interested speaker.
3. You should strongly desire to stimulate the thinking and reactions of your audience.
4. You should be intent upon accomplishing the goal you have chosen for your speech and eager to share your thoughts and experiences with your listeners.

5. You should be active, full of life and vigor—not passive, inhibited, or unwilling to "let yourself go."
6. You should be friendly, pleasant, and courteous.

Personal Characteristics and Behavior—Your personal characteristics must be attractive to the audience. They like to see you well groomed, wearing clothes appropriate for the occasion. If you are sincerely speaking to project to your classmates, dress as you choose. How will you choose?

The audience likes your conduct on the platform to be in good taste, friendly, courteous, and well mannered. They like to see you poised and dignified, exhibiting mastery of yourself and of the situation and showing confidence in your success, but not giving impressions of overconfidence, smugness, or conceit. Audiences like a speaker who is actively interested, energetic, and excitedly alive, but not tense and nervous; who is rather relaxed and comfortable, but not unconcerned or careless.

They want to hear and understand easily. They will, if your voice is pleasing and sufficiently loud, but not so loud as to call attention to itself. They want your pronunciation to be sufficiently correct to be acceptable and sufficiently distinct to be easily understood; your language, in addition to expressing your ideas clearly, in good taste; your bodily activity integrated with the thought and feeling as you express it and appropriate to the situation, not full of distracting random movements.

Audiences gain impressions from the moment you first appear until you retire. Hence, when you are seated on the platform, they prefer to see you sit straight, usually with your legs uncrossed. When you are introduced by the chairman, rise, acknowledge the chairman with a nod and a smile perhaps, and proceed to the speaker's stand or near the center of the platform. Take a position before beginning to speak, pause, address the chairman and audience, and look directly at your audience as you speak your first sentence rather slowly, distinctly, and loudly enough to be heard easily. At the conclusion of your speech pause, take a step backward, walk to your seat, stop, face the front, pause, and sit down. Do not fall or slump into your seat. Keep your eyes on the chairman and audience for a moment, then relax, but sit erect and be inconspicuous.

Communicate with Energy and Enthusiasm—You should be communicative. Speak with "a lively sense of communication," that is, with:

1. an eagerness that is exhilarating,
2. a natural enjoyment that is charming and catching,
3. an evident but spontaneous muscular energy that is enlivening,
4. a released inherent enthusiasm that is contagious,
5. a sincerity and earnestness that are unquestionably convincing,
6. a depth of belief that is persuasive,

7. an emphasis and force that are irresistible, and
8. a warmth that is personal.

Amplified Conversation—To be communicative, you must be conversational, but let your speaking manner be that of amplified conversation. In one sense, it should be loud conversation. Whatever constitutes polite conversation when amplified to fit the situation is the basis of communicativeness. Remember that when you make a speech, it is to a number of people as an audience. Hence, the conversational manner suited to the "drawing room" simply will not do on the public platform. You are warned therefore that you cannot project well if you are too conversational, too quiet, or too easy. Your speaking manner must be sufficiently intense to stimulate the listener's complete attention.

Make it a point to talk *to* your audience, not *at* them. Speak each idea directly to them as if it were a personal matter. Look at them. Face them. Keep direct eye contact with them. Avoid a constant "looking-about" from side to side, to floor, to ceiling, to speaker's stand while you are speaking. Not only will this mannerism annoy the audience, but it will also cause you to lose their attention.

Adapting to Changing Conditions in the Situation—To please your audience, you would do well to adapt your speech (as it develops), your style of presenting it, your behavior, and your manner to changing conditions in the situation. Your audience will respond with their attention in spite of distracting and disturbing factors which may occur. Sometimes their attention will lag. If it does, you must regain it. Sometimes you can do this by being more intense in projection. Sometimes it is necessary to introduce more and perhaps different but related illustrations, anecdotes, instances, and circumstances than you had originally planned to use. They must be especially interesting and stimulating to the immediate audience.

If the audience is uncomfortable, what can you do? If the ventilation of the room is bad, have doors and windows opened, if possible. If the audience appears to be suffering from the cold and windows are open, have them closed, if convenient. If the program has already been long and the members of the audience seem tired and restless, some speakers have them rise, stretch, and relax, or they use some other method to accomplish the same result where the situation will permit it. If persons are standing in the room and seats are available, you might ask them to be seated before you begin your speech. Speak loudly enough so that all may hear easily. If the audience is extremely fatigued, listless, or uncomfortable, shorten your speech rather than continue at length under such circumstances.

Audiences are affected by disturbing factors—When things happen, your audience will respond favorably to you if you give evidence that you have complete control of the situation, that you are not irritated or upset. If a sudden humorous incident occurs, laugh with the audience. Allow them to respond to the incident fully, then turn the incident to your advantage, if possible. If sudden noises occur, such as train whistles, a passing fire engine, shouting, and the like, pause for a time, perhaps comment upon the disturbance, repeat your last sentence or two, then continue. If certain members of the audience "heckle" or interrupt you, respond with sincerity, good nature, and good taste, turning the incident to your advantage and thereby increasing the sympathy of the audience toward you. If your audience evidences coldness, prejudice, or enmity toward you, win them, if possible, by a direct appeal for fair play and open-mindedness. Sometimes you may effectively use an indirect approach in which you present inherently interesting facts, anecdotes, or comments which are in themselves absorbing and stimulating and which capture attention.

If you make errors or incorrect statements or have trouble in getting under way or in saying what you mean, make the correction that should be made, perhaps beg the pardon of the audience or make some other appropriate comment, and proceed. Do not allow yourself to be disturbed if such things occur.

The audience will like it if you give the impression that what you do and the way you do it arises naturally out of the situation, your idea, your feelings, and their reactions.

Speak Up! Speak Up! Speak Up!   This is the key to effective communication with an audience. It takes energy. It is characteristic of enthusiasm. It gets and holds attention. It is one of the first and most important speaking habits for you to acquire.

19   *Control of Bodily Activity*

Bodily Action While Speaking Is a Natural Occurrence—It is not an artificial technique to be acquired, to be used only by flowery orators. It is an inherent skill that you yourself possess. Bodily action while speaking, both gross and refined, occurs as you project your thoughts and feelings to your listeners. It arises from those thoughts and feelings, as well as from the reactions of your immediate audience.

Under normal conditions, in simple speaking situations where ordinary conversation occurs, bodily activity is natural in the act of speaking and is adequate. In public speaking situations, however, it must be kept under constant control and used objectively and purposefully.

Though bodily action is naturally involved in projection to the audience, its importance in speech making warrants its emphasis as a separate technique in the total process of stimulating an adequate audience response. Hence, control of bodily activity is treated here separately as an essential of speech making.

Importance of Experience—Use bodily activity freely from the very beginning of your practice in speech making. Use it with abandon. Have little concern, for a time, about "how you look" or whether the action is appropriate—just use it. Lose all of your inhibitions and self-consciousness as soon as possible.

The first step is to release the bodily action that is natural for you and that you hesitate to use because of lack of experience. The second step is to learn to control that action and make it purposive. In other words, your first job is to become able to use your own natural gestures comfortably when you want to use them before an audience, rather than to be concerned about when, how, or how well you use them. You will discover that if you follow this advice you will receive very little criticism and that you will need very little instruction in bodily action. Suggestions from your speech teacher may be helpful to you, but they cannot substitute for extended experience in making gestures while making speeches.

It should be very clear to you that effective bodily action is more a product of wide and varied experience as a speaker than of specific instruction or drill.

The Whole Body—The human body is a whole. It functions as a whole. It functions best as a whole. Its nature and condition not only influence, but may actually determine its behavior continuously or at a given moment. For example, the type and extent of action used by men while speaking is quite different from that used by women. Men customarily use more action and broader and more forceful action than women.

Bodily activity includes posture, movement, gesture, and facial expression. All are simultaneously related to the thought and feeling of the speaker at the moment. Each is dependent upon the other. Though they may be studied separately, they must, nevertheless, be considered as a whole.

Movements of the parts of the body—the arms, hands, legs, head, face, eyes—arise from, individuate out of, and are a refinement of total or gross bodily movement. A program of individual training in control of bodily activity might best proceed, therefore, as follows:

1. development of appropriate posture;
2. control of gross bodily movement—walking, broad gesturing;
3. techniques of platform movement—controlling bodily weight, use of legs and feet;
4. techniques in the use of the arms and hands to stimulate the listener and the audience to respond most completely;

5. control of head movements;
6. control of facial expression; and
7. control of eye movements.

Control Posture—You should have a good posture. The position of your body, standing or sitting, should allow your muscles to function normally and with ease. There is no single posture suited to all speakers but you should be guided by the following: Your posture should be comfortable. The muscles of your body should not be stiff or tense while speaking. They should instead be comfortably relaxed. Your posture should aid you in looking your best. Good posture is the basis of poise. It is an important factor in the impression that you make on your audience. Your posture should facilitate a free and easy functioning of your breathing mechanism and facilitate free and easy bodily movements in walking about the platform and in gesturing.

Experiment with the following in developing your best possible platform speaking posture:

1. Stand tall!
2. Stand on both feet with your weight equally balanced between them.
3. Keep your legs straight but not stiff, your knees relaxed.
4. Keep your shoulder, back, and neck muscles relaxed—free from strain and tenseness.
5. Allow your arms and hands to hang naturally at your sides.
6. Have your head up and your chin in, with no tenseness.

You should avoid the following:

1. standing with too wide a base, your feet wide apart.
2. throwing your weight completely on one leg, thereby appearing unbalanced.
3. leaning from your waist toward the audience.
4. leaning backward with your weight on your heels.
5. folding your arms across your chest.
6. holding your arms tightly behind your back.
7. placing your hands on your hips.
8. keeping your hands in your pockets continuously.

Control Bodily Movement—You should control your bodily movement. You may wish to move about the platform. Such movement is probably wise if occasioned by the situation. You may desire to change your position so as to relax, rest yourself, rest your audience, and increase the attention of your audience. You may desire to change your position to indicate transition of thought at the completion of the development of a portion of your speech. You may wish to move toward the audience in order to be more emphatic.

If you move, you should do it gracefully but naturally. You should step first with the leg toward the direction in which you are moving. Your weight before you move should be carried by the other leg. Make your movements decisive. Do not creep or side-step when you want to walk about the platform. Take natural, positive steps. Avoid unmotivated movement about the platform, movement that is not occasioned by the situation. Avoid mechanical movements that appear to be planned—so many steps one way, so many steps another. When in doubt, stand still.

Control Gestures—You may wish to use gestures. Effective gestures will aid you in projecting your ideas. Gestures help to get and hold attention. Since the arms and hands are the principal agents of gesture, you should note the following:

1. Your gestures should be in harmony with the thoughts and feelings that you express. They should vary in nature, duration, and intensity as your thoughts and feelings vary.
2. Your gestures should supplement adequately the vocal expression of your thoughts and feelings. They should not be overdone, neither should they be slighted. Each gesture should be a full gesture, completed and finished. Your hand and arm should not be just held up, then dropped. Let your gesture actually aid you in expressing your thought and feeling.
3. Begin your gesture "of the moment" as you begin speaking the thought to which it is related. Let it develop as that thought and the feeling associated with it develops. Let the gesture actually help to focus and hold the attention of the listener. This will aid you in being clear, being emphatic and in bringing the expression of your thought and feeling to a climax.
4. Your hand and arm gestures should be natural, graceful, free, and easy. They should be smooth and rhythmical rather than abrupt and jerky. Each gesture should seem to flow into the next.

When your gestures are natural, the whole arm should be used and should be used as a whole. That is, as the speaker uses his whole arm, the listener should not notice movements of the shoulder, elbow, wrist, or fingers separately. Although the whole arm is used, it should not be completely extended in gesturing. Some restraint should always be used. The shoulder, elbow, wrist, and fingers should be relaxed and flexible, not tense or stiff. Movements of the hand and arm should proceed away from the center of the body. Hand and arm movements should follow curved lines—the wrist should lead the hand.

Practice the use of the basic types of "hands" in gesturing.

The pointing hand—The index finger is straight and strong; the rest of the hand is clenched somewhat tightly. This "hand" is used for directing attention to ideas as well as things. It is used to identify, to indicate location, and to give a sense of direction. It is used to "point up" as well as to emphasize. This type of gesture is usually an active one, often vigorous. The finger and hand should not just be held up and then dropped. Both hands are not used simultaneously.

The giving hand—The "hand" is open, palm up. The fingers are fully extended. This "hand" is used in giving and receiving symbolically as well as actually. You give or take an idea as you give or take an object. This "hand" may accompany generalizations, appeals, interrogations, requests for consideration, attitudes of agreement, or the making of admissions. It is sometimes used to suggest enclosing, encircling, or encompassing. Both hands, right and left, are used in coordination, sometimes simultaneously. This "hand" is not usually a vigorous gesture, but it is an active one.

The covering hand—Like the giving hand, this "hand" is open and the fingers are fully extended, but the palm is down. The speaker may use this "hand" to indicate covering, quieting, subduing, pressing down, putting down, things beneath, encompassing, or saying "no, no." It is not usually a vigorous gesture. Both hands may be used coordinately and simultaneously.

The repelling hand—This "hand" is open and bent up at the wrist, with fingers fully extended and the palm toward the audience. It pushes away, repels, gets rid of, denies, forbids, nullifies, abrogates, cuts off or cuts down, abhors, protects, or protests. It is an active gesture, vigorous at times, with either hand used occasionally and sometimes both simultaneously.

The clenched hand—This "hand" is a closed fist. It is the most vigorous of gestures and expresses the strongest feelings. It pounds for emphasis, exhibits strength and force, and indicates opposition. It may symbolize courage, determination, anger, hatred, or revenge. One or both hands are used. It is an active gesture.

You may use your hands in gesturing in ways other than those described above, but for the most part your "hands" will be of these specific types or will be variations closely identified with one or more of them.

If you rehearse these types of "hands" appropriately, improved habits of gesturing can result. Your gestures may thus become less random and careless. Mannerisms, if you have them, will tend to be minimized or eliminated. With improved habits in the use of the basic types of "hands," your gestures will tend to be more objective and meaningful. You, as a person, will appear more coordinated, more poised, and more refined.

The danger is that in rehearsing these "hands" improperly your gesturing habits may come to be mechanical. You can avoid the mechanical by using a practice method which permits you to grow into the new habit instead of trying to acquire it all at once. In such a method, you practice first the gross or general form of the gesture. Then, through criticism and further practice accordingly, you refine the particular gesture into natural behavior for you.

Control Head Movements and Facial Expression—Head movements and facial expression are inherent in the act of speaking. They are spontaneous, natural, and adequate when the speaker is uninhibited. During speech making they may need to be controlled.

Head movements—Your head movements (front to back, side to side, rotating) in speech making, to be effective, must be used selectively and purposefully. They should not be random movements. They should be coordinated with your bodily movements and your hand and arm gestures. Your head movements can aid you in focusing attention, in expressing meaning, and in being emphatic. As in the case of your hand and arm gestures, your head movements must be timed just right.

Facial expression—Your facial expression can be a major factor in your effectiveness. If you do not have a mobile face, if you are habitually "dead-pan," you should develop facial flexibility to the extent that it readily reflects in a natural way your thoughts and feelings and supplements strongly their vocal expression. To be effective, your facial expressions must be clearly and completely meaningful but not conspicuous in themselves. They must be purposeful, spontaneous, natural, and suited to your face and personality. They must not be random, meaningless, or out of harmony with what you are saying. Controlled facial expression helps to focus and hold the listener's attention. It adds depth, richness, and personal intensity and vitality to the vocal and bodily expression of your thought and feeling.

Although facial expression should be developed as a whole, you should give specific attention to the use of your eyes, your brows, and your lips. You should be certain that they are responsive to the mood, feeling, and emotional aspects of what you say as you say it. If not, practice to make them so. Also, be certain that you have no mannerisms of facial movement that will prevent them from responding freely to your thought and feeling as you experience it.

Sometimes it is a good idea to practice in front of a mirror, to study and experiment with your facial movements as you speak. Practice a smile now and then. Audiences like to look at speakers who seem to be pleased to be speaking.

It is best to have your face as well lighted as possible while you are speaking in order that your facial expressions can be easily seen by the audience as well as appropriately highlighted to insure full effectiveness.

Adapt to the Speaking Situation—You should adapt your bodily activity to the speaking situation and control it accordingly. The more informal the situation, the more informal your behavior should be, but always within the requirements of good taste. The more formal the situation, the more formal your behavior should be, but avoid being too formal.

The kind of action needed will vary with your audience and the auditorium. Broad action is required for large mixed audiences and more refined action for smaller, more select audiences. The amount of action needed will vary with your audience, its size, its physical condition (fatigued, fidgety, and so forth), its emotional state (sympathetic, prejudiced, and so forth), and your own emotional state. Use more action for large, fatigued, or prejudiced audiences or on festive occasions. But use less action for small, alert audiences or for audiences gathered on solemn occasions. Usually, as tension increases, you use a greater amount of action and use it with more intensity. Use neither too much nor too little in any case. Keep yourself under control and use gestures selectively.

Common Faults—You should beware of certain common faults in using bodily action: You should avoid unmotivated action—action that has no reason or purpose. Unmotivated action detracts from your effectiveness. Action should aid you in projection of thought and feeling or be omitted. You should, as a rule, avoid extreme or unusual action. Keep some reserve. You should avoid gesturing with the forearm only or with the elbows close to the body. You should avoid indefinite, continuous movement and gesture, such as flipping your hands or pawing the air. Make your gestures specific, clear-cut, and decisive or omit them. You should avoid giving the appearance of gesturing at stated intervals, of using a gesture because it is in a good place and because you think you ought to use it there or because you rehearsed it there. You should avoid gesturing across your body. Use your right hand for gestures to the right, your left for gestures to the left.

You should avoid certain annoying mannerisms which may detract from your effectiveness: playing with your clothes—pockets, buttons, necklace, necktie, handkerchief; playing with objects—notecards, pencils, rings, watch chains, pens, keys, money, the chair, the speaker's stand, the desk; playing with your hands or your fingers; stumbling, shuffling your feet as you walk, bumping into furniture; looking out the window, at the ceiling, or at the floor (semiprofile positions); pacing the floor. Don't appear restless by rising on your toes or heels continuously or swaying back and forth. Do not use stereotyped gestures and never use the same gestures over and over again.

20 Rhythm

Rhythm in speech making refers to the flow of the speaker's thought and language through vocal presentation. A speaker who is superior in rhythm speaks fluently, smoothly, and effortlessly; there is a "forward-moving" continuity in his thought and language. At the other extreme is the one who speaks with effort and, regardless of how hard he tries, is unable to make his speech mechanism function with a "forward-moving" continuity. He lacks the timing necessary for the integration of its parts.

Inadequacies—Listeners become aware of and are disturbed by the following inadequacies: jerky, irregular speaking characterized by the repetition of sounds, syllables, words, and even whole phrases; unusual pauses and hesitation inappropriate as to place, frequency, and length of occurrence; vocalizing of pauses in which the sound "uh-uh-uh" or "ah-ah-ah" occurs (during hesitations, "uh" or "ah" is sometimes added to words, resulting in such vocalizations as "he-uh," "they-uh," "well-uh," "and-uh," "for-uh"); voice patterns of pitch, intensity, and rate in which identical voice inflections are repeated regardless of the thought being formulated; sudden utterance of phrases, words, syllables, or sounds that are unnatural and inappropriate at the moment.

If your speaking is characterized by any of these inadequacies, your effectiveness cannot help but be noticeably impaired. Your awareness of them is necessary for the most rapid improvement. It is important to recognize that you can improve the effect of your speaking by making it more fluent.

What to Avoid—Improve the rhythm of your speaking and aid its "forward-moving" flow by learning to avoid certain common manifestations of poor rhythm:

1. Avoid speaking more slowly or rapidly than is normal for you.
2. Avoid sudden and unwarranted changes in your rate of speaking and the intensity and pitch of your voice.
3. Avoid using more intensity on the first syllable of a word or the first word of a phrase or sentence than on the remainder, unless necessary for emphasis.
4. Avoid starting or ending all words, phrases, and sentences at the same pitch level.

5. Avoid consistent repetition of the same variation of pitch, intensity, and rate of speaking and the continuous use of the same inflections regardless of meaning. An example of the continuous use of the same voice inflections is often called "singsong" rhythm.
6. Avoid adding the sound "uh" on the end of words, such as "and-uh," "well-uh."
7. Avoid vocalizing during pauses, for example saying "uh-uh-uh" or "ah-ah-ah" while you are trying to find the right word or formulate the next thought unit.

Breathing Important—Check the effectiveness of your breathing while speaking. You should satisfy each of the following requirements. If you are unable to do so, you should practice until you can. These breathing skills are not only vital to fluency in speech making but also basic to adequacy in phonation and articulation.

1. You should be able to fill your lungs adequately either quickly or slowly.
2. You should be able to fill your lungs adequately without fatigue.
3. You should be able to exhale quickly or slowly as necessary.
4. You should be able to suspend and resume inspiration and expiration at will.
5. You should be able to sustain sounds or speak for a time on an ordinary breath.
6. You should be able to inhale quietly, noiselessly, and as often as necessary.
7. You should be able to maintain a reserve supply of breath.
8. You should be able to breathe naturally without the awareness of the audience and to breathe without gasping.
9. You should be able to breathe without interfering with the muscular processes operating in the formation of sound.

Knowledge and Preparation Vital—You cannot speak fluently on a subject that you know little or nothing about. Neither can you speak fluently when your speech is inadequately prepared. You must choose subjects about which you have intimate knowledge, which are in the realm of your experience, and with which you feel "at home." Your subjects should be of the kind that you strongly desire to talk about, subjects that you will enjoy sharing with your listeners.

You must be sure of what you are going to say and how you are going to say it. You must carefully and thoroughly prepare each speech. You must be completely familiar with your material, its organization, and how you are going to develop each thought. You should not be "at a loss" as to what comes next. You must have thought about your speech, worked over it, and lived with it long enough to know it well.

Develop Speaking Readiness—Readiness to speak at one's best, regardless of the situation, requires a natural self-control of the functioning of the total bodily mechanism. This control makes for constancy and steadiness in the functioning of the speech mechanism. A constant and steady functioning of the speech mechanism makes for speaking that is fluent and effortless and that seems to flow forward with a spontaneous, easy-to-listen-to movement. Such speaking rates high in rhythm.

It should be pointed out that the greatest deterrents to speaking readiness are emotional instability, excitement, nervousness, tenseness, and stage fright. All upset the normal rhythm of your bodily and speech mechanism and cause it to function abnormally.

We indicated above that you will be more fluent in speech making if you avoid the more obvious characteristics of poor rhythm, if you have or develop good habits of breathing while speaking, if you speak on subjects within the range of your own personal experience, and if you are always thoroughly prepared. These immediate approaches to improvement in rhythm should be accompanied by a longer-range goal—speaking readiness.

To acquire this speaking readiness, with its spontaneous, natural, and forward-moving flow of utterance, be guided by the following:

Be relaxed, composed, confident, and poised—Learn to keep your body relaxed, your feelings composed, and your attitude confident during speech making. Each speech presentation should begin with a positive mental attitude which causes you to behave accordingly. Get started well by thinking about what you have to say, immediately before you are called upon and while you are speaking, rather than worrying about yourself, how you will do, or how you are doing. You should say the first sentence over to yourself several times immediately before you are introduced, in order to have it clearly in mind and hence get off to a good start.

Take your time while you are speaking. Pause when necessary to visualize and formulate your next thought. Maintain an outward appearance of ease and relaxation.

Speak often—Take every opportunity to practice speaking to others. Through experience, you will increase your facility for speaking. Speak to all kinds of audiences in all kinds of situations. Also attend social gatherings as often as possible and participate actively as a conversationalist. Speak impromptu; speak from prepared notes; read aloud at sight as well as from familiar materials; recite poetry and prose from memory. If you do not have enough real audiences to practice on, speak to imaginary ones.

Hear good speakers—Take every opportunity possible to hear accomplished professional speakers. Keep yourself relaxed while you listen and put yourself in accord with the spontaneously fluent, "forward-moving flow" of the speakers' thought and language. The influence on your speech will be indirect and subtle, but nevertheless can be very marked.

Broaden your vocabulary—With more words at the "tip of your tongue," greater fluency is not only possible but probable.

21   Pronunciation

Characteristics—Pronunciation refers to the way sounds, syllables, and words are spoken in continuous speech. For your pronunciation to be acceptable, your spoken words should be pronounced as a majority of the respected people who hear you would pronounce them themselves. For your pronunciation to be superior, it should also be free of provincialisms and substandard regionalisms.

You should keep in mind that the section of the country makes a difference in the way some words are pronounced. Students of pronunciation have pointed out that in general there are three principal types of pronunciation in the United States—Eastern, Southern, and General American. By far, they say, the largest number of us are accustomed to General American pronunciations.

Some words have more than one acceptable pronunciation, though one may be preferable. Pronunciations may change with time, even from generation to generation. Uncommon, unusual, and unfamiliar pronunciations must be avoided wherever you speak. In case of doubt, you should find out what pronunciations are recommended by consulting recent standard dictionaries. Learn to use these pronunciations regularly.

Acceptable pronunciation—Technically, to meet the qualifications of acceptable pronunciation, the speaker must choose the proper sounds, combine them appropriately into syllables and words, speak the sounds and syllables correctly and accurately, and give each syllable within the word its proper stress. Thus for your pronunciation to be acceptable, it must conform to the following specific qualifications:

Your speech sounds should be formed correctly and accurately. Inaccurate, careless, or slovenly formation of the speech sounds is responsible for most inadequate pronunciations. The correct speech sounds should be used in their proper place and order. For example, avoid the use of incorrect vowels—[gɪt] (get), [dʒɪst] (just). Avoid the use of incorrect consonants—[əsɛpt] (accept), [wɪtʃ] (which), [lɪbərdɪ] (liberty), [lɛnθ] (length). Avoid the addition of sounds—[draʊndɛd] (drowned), [ɪlənɔɪz] (Illinois), [ətæktɛd] (attacked), [lɔr] (law). Avoid the insertion of sounds—[ondlɪ] (only), [stəstɪstɪks] (statistics), [æθəlɛtɪk] (athletic). Avoid the transposition of sounds—[pɪrdɪ] (pretty), [prɛspɪreɪʃən] (perspiration). Avoid omitting necessary sounds—[gʌvərmənt] (government), [fɛbjuɛrɪ] (February), [dʒɛnlmən] (gentlemen).

Each word should be spoken with its proper accent or proper syllabic stress. For example, avoid overstressing unstressed syllables—['diːpɑrtmənt] (depart'ment), ['diːtrɔɪt] (Detroit'). Avoid misplacing accent or stress—[θi'eɪtr] (theater), [supɪr'fluəs] (superfluous), ['polis] (police').

Obsolete, local, colloquial, vulgar, and dialect pronunciations should not be used except to produce desired effects.

Adapt Your Pronunciation—You should pronounce your words especially slowly, forming the syllables and consonants especially precisely when speaking to large audiences in large auditoriums, when speaking in auditoriums where the hearing conditions are uncertain, when speaking in noisy situations, and when your thought is especially significant and you wish to draw attention to it.

Use of Dialects—When using dialects in storytelling, your pronunciations should conform to the character types and the era and locality in which they lived or from which they came. It is better to suggest dialect pronunciations than to reproduce them exactly. If a dialect is spoken too exactly, the audience may not be able to understand what you say.

22   Voice Control

Voice Control, a Special Skill—Voice, like bodily activity, is essential to the projection to the listener of the speaker's thought and feeling. Effective speakers rate high in projection to the audience. The most effective speakers also rate high in voice control.

When you speak spontaneously in everyday situations, your voice tends to express your thoughts and feelings adequately. However, when you are making a speech to an audience, you are most effective when your voice points up for the listener, in more than just a casual way, the inner, deeper, richer meanings of your thoughts and feelings. This pointing up requires an objective and conscious control of your voice—its pitch, intensity, duration, and quality. Through effective voice control, you gain and hold your listener's attention more readily, you make your meanings clearer and sharper, and you give them greater depth, making your meanings more vivid and stimulating to the listener. Of course, this conscious and objective control of your voice, to be effective, cannot be obvious or mechanical. It should seem habitual and natural.

Development of Voice Control—Effectiveness in voice control is developed through experience in speaking and reading aloud, voice training, and persistent directed practice. This training and practice, to be of value, must be in terms of specific voice skills needed in speech making.

Experience in speaking—Through experience in speech making and reading aloud, you become aware of the need for voice control. You learn what it does and what it can do for you in enriching your speaking effectiveness. You become especially alert to the nature of audience attention and reactions to voice changes and inflections.

Voice training—You must learn to recognize variations in your own voice—its pitch, intensity, duration, and quality. Your ear should detect subtle as well as broad changes and inflections. Ear training is the first step in the development of voice control skills.

Experiment with the functioning of your vocal mechanism—Become aware of the kinds of sounds, tones, and noises that it will produce. Produce these various kinds again and again until your mind and ear and vocal mechanism are so coordinated that when a specific sound or tone or noise is wanted the mechanism adjusts to produce it automatically.

Four basic types of experiments are especially helpful in developing voice control in speech making:

1. Experimentation with pitch level, pitch range, and pitch inflection. Involved are adjustments within the larynx, principally of the vocal cords. Proper and sufficient experimentation results in clearer, more exact, more pointed, and more subtle expression of the nature, the depth, and the intricacy of your thought and feeling. This fineness of expression, made possible by controlled pitch modulations, results in easier and more attentive listening. The opposite is the result of inadequate control of pitch.

2. Experimentation with the size and shape of the mouth, throat, and nasal cavities and the openings to and from each. The soft palate, the tongue, the lips, the cheeks, and the lower jaw are all involved in one way or another in voice control, affecting especially voice quality and intensity. The quality of your voice can become nasal, denasal, muffled, metallic, harsh, hoarse-husky, breathy, or infantile, as well as clear and pleasant, depending on the way you adjust the size and shape of the throat and nasal cavities and the openings to and from each. You will amaze yourself at what you can do with your voice in producing various types of voice quality. If you have a weak voice, proper adjustment of these cavities may help to make it stronger.

3. Experimentation with breath pressure in voice production. Your experimentation should result in: (a) precision in the initiation of the necessary breath pressure to start the production of vocal tones of the required strength or intensity; (b) precision in stopping vocal

tones through discontinuing breath pressure; (c) ease in maintaining steady breath pressure, weak or strong, in the production of vocal tones for long or short periods as necessary; (d) the ability to increase or decrease the intensity of a tone during its production.

4. Experimentation with the duration of the tones of your voice. Your experimenting should develop your ability to: (a) hold constant the size and shape of the cavities and their openings as long as necessary to produce vocal tones of the required duration, intensity, and quality; (b) hold constant the necessary breath pressure in relation to the adjustment of the cavities and their openings to produce vocal tones of the required duration, intensity, and quality; (c) change quickly or slowly the size and shape of the cavities and their openings and the required related breath pressures to produce easily but accurately the variations in duration, intensity, and quality of tone which are required to express the speaker's thought.

Voice Control Skills—Experimentation with your voice should lead to your acquiring certain skills:

1. the use of your total pitch range;
2. ability to vary pitch within syllables, sounds, and words;
3. ability to use rising and falling inflections;
4. ability to use your total range of intensity;
5. ability to vary intensity within sounds, words, and syllables;
6. ability to build up intensity—or diminish it;
7. ability to use longer or shorter duration of sound on words or syllables;
8. ability to vary the length of pauses at will;
9. ability to vary voice quality at will;
10. ability to reproduce rhythm patterns, inflectional changes, and quality characteristics of people and dialects.

V THE ESSENTIAL SKILLS
OF READING ALOUD

Introduction

There are two basic kinds of speaking: original and interpretative. In original speaking the speaker presents his own ideas to an audience, whereas in interpretative speaking (reading aloud) the speaker presents the ideas of another, in the words of the author, and interprets their meaning as completely as possible or as may be necessary for the immediate audience. Although the ideas and words are those of another, the speaker's interpretation is his own; that is, it is based upon his own understanding of and his own experience in relation to what the author has written and the response he wishes to secure from his immediate audience. As in original speaking, the speaker must first get the attention and interest of the listener; second, he must hold that attention and interest throughout his presentation; third, he must make his and the author's thoughts and feelings clear so that the listener will understand and appreciate them; and fourth, through the manner of his presentation, he must fix these thoughts and feelings in the mind of the listener so that they may be recalled readily. And these demands on the reader hold wherever he may read—at a business meeting, at home, at church, or as a professional public performer.

Essentials of Interpretative Reading—As in original speaking, there are essentials for study and practice in developing skill in reading aloud. These essentials, similar for the most part to those in original speaking, are:

1. Choice of Material
2. Arrangement of Material
3. Projection of Thought
4. Projection of Emotion
5. Control of Bodily Activity
6. Rhythm
7. Pronunciation and
8. Voice Control.

23   *Choice of Material*

Material Suited to the Reader—When you are considering selections of prose and poetry for reading aloud, ask yourself whether the selection in question is suited to you personally. Is it within the range of your own experience? Do you understand it? Can you visualize the author's meaning? Do you appreciate its inner, deeper, richer meanings? Can you interpret effectively for the audience the thoughts, moods, and emotions involved, as well as the characters, if any are included? Is it too difficult for you to read at this time? Do you have the time to rehearse it to read it well? Do you really want to read the selection? Will you enjoy doing it, if you can read it well? How much time will you have for the reading? What is your place on the program, if there is more than one reader?

It may be that you have done very little reading aloud before taking this course. In that event, be especially careful in selecting material that suits you. You may wish to experiment with several types of material—and there is no place better to do it than the classroom.

Material Suited to the Audience and the Occasion—Be certain that what you would like to read is suited to the audience and to the occasion. As in original speaking, you must analyze your probable audience in terms of its composition (age, common interests, intellectual and emotional levels, likes and dislikes, probable mood and behavior), its probable attitude toward you, the occasion for the meeting, recent events, and what will please the audience especially.

Again you might think of your classroom. Generally speaking, your classmates are much like you, with similar interests and backgrounds. So try things out on them and check their response.

Long and Short Selections—In deciding upon suitable material in terms of your time limit, you may find it best to read a cutting from a long selection or two or more selections written by the same or different authors which, because of a common theme or mood, can appropriately be presented in one performance. But never choose a selection for the one reason that it is suited to the time limit.

24   Arrangement of Material

Frequently the material you use will have to be adapted, rearranged, cut, and edited to best accomplish your purpose. Before reading the selection, you will usually find it necessary to do some or all of the following: give the title of the material; tell who wrote it; make selected, interesting comments about the author; give the reasons why the material is being read or what the selection is supposed to illustrate; furnish background material to arouse interest; supply the time, place, and setting, if it is a story; clarify unusual expressions or characters.

If you use several selections, you may build them around a theme which is made clear at the beginning. Arrange them in the order that develops the theme most satisfactorily and, as you progress, relate one selection to another and to the theme by appropriate transitional remarks.

Introductory Remarks—It is best to provide an appropriate introduction to the selection you are going to read. It will give your audience an opportunity to become accustomed to your manner of speaking before you begin to read, as well as give you an opportunity to become acquainted with your audience and to adjust to the situation.

In your introduction, make any necessary explanations about the selection to be read, perhaps reviewing its historical background or supplying information about unusual circumstances or events that are related to the reading. If you have chosen to make a cutting from a long selection, you will certainly include in the introduction a synopsis of the events that precede the particular episode you are about to read.

Frequently, by your comments at the beginning, you can point up the theme, the impression, the mood, or the universal appeal of the selection you are about to read. You might decide to talk about the author himself, that is, to give a brief biographical sketch, to discuss his personality, or to analyze his style of writing. Or you might prefer to explain why the selection appeals to you or why you decided to read it on this occasion.

In short, your introduction provides an appropriate setting for your reading, facilitates understanding and appreciation by the listeners, and disposes them favorably toward you and the reading that is to follow.

Cutting Material—Frequently you may desire to read a selection which is too long for the time allowed. Often such material can, by proper cutting, be made to fit the time, the audience, and the occasion. There are excellent poems, short stories, plays, and novels which, after being carefully cut, can become excellent reading material.

After carefully studying the selection, with a full understanding of the theme and its development, pencil out the unnecessary or nonessential parts. Undoubtedly, it will be necessary to add words or phrases or even sentences in various places to knit the story together, to bridge the gaps occasioned by your cutting, and to insure proper sequence and unity. After you have made the cutting, read the remaining selection aloud completely to determine what else is needed in the way of connecting words. Write in these words or expressions and revise them until the selection reads easily and smoothly. Reread the selection aloud as a whole and continue the process of editing until the selection has unity and coherence and contains all the essential material, but only that which is necessary to the full development of the author's theme. Be careful not to destroy or diminish the author's contribution. The final cutting should be a complete, finished unit in itself, not a series of excerpts which are obviously patched together.

We recommend the following steps and procedures:

1. Carefully read through the entire selection.

2. Identify and think through its principal points; condense these points into an outline for your guidance in making the cutting.

3. Now reread the entire selection, pencilling out nonessential portions, especially long expositions or descriptions.

4. In some cases you will choose one incident from a longer selection. This episode must become a complete unit in itself. After you have arranged your introduction, what precedes or follows the incident in the original should not be necessary to give it unity.

5. In many instances, you may find that you are able to omit entire pages, chapters, or incidents. You will retain coherence by weaving in a few transitional sentences of your own to carry the story along when parts have been omitted. Occasionally it may be necessary to write in a few sentences for a character in the story to speak in words consistent with his characterization.

6. Next, study the dialogue with a view to omitting any unnecessary

passages. Most of the time you will find that you can omit the "he said," or "she answered" explanations of the author. You can make the characters identifiable through vocal change or head position.

7. If there are many characters, delete those who are unimportant or unnecessary in developing the story, scene, or incident. Occasionally, it may be necessary to reassign speeches originally intended for another person, and perhaps to rephrase them somewhat. If you have a scene in which two people speak, do not hesitate to combine two or three short speeches of a single character into one longer speech, omitting the interrupting comments of the second character.

Cutting a play—In cutting a play the same general rules apply, but remember to give the setting, the time, the place, and the circumstances and to describe the characters. The playwright frequently supplies you with the proper words with which to "set" each scene and act.

In cutting a play, strive to retain theatrical expressions, for example, "As the scene opens, there is a light knock at the door. Barrie's voice is heard calling Susan, his wife."

You might end a scene in some such way as this, "Barrie lets the roses fall slowly at Susan's feet. She looks at him with untold wonder as the curtain falls on Act One."

For years the late Burns Mantle and other recorders of the activity of the American theater have prepared shortened versions of the best plays of the year. Mantle carefully deleted portions of the script and added comments of his own, so that in perhaps twenty-five or thirty pages a faithful representation of the play was presented. Your problem is much the same, except that where Mantle presented the entire play, which would take nearly an hour to read, you will present only a scene or, at the most, one act.

Cutting a novel—The cutting of a novel offers a few special problems, the foremost of which is the retention of unity and plot sequence. Constantly keep in mind the development of the theme or thesis on which the novel is based.

Other suggestions made previously definitely apply to the novel, such as the elimination of unnecessary characters, the deletion of long expository and descriptive passages, and the rewriting of some narration into dialogue. If you choose to omit whole passages and to concentrate on one major episode (which is easier than cutting a whole novel), you will need to be extremely careful in working out your introduction to the selection so that the audience may be properly prepared for what is to follow.

Cutting an oration or speech—Review the previous general suggestions on cutting. In cutting an oration or speech, you have a choice between two methods: you may retain the original as a whole and omit those portions which are not absolutely essential to the development of the central idea; or you may decide to take only a portion, perhaps only one major point in the oration, and present it in its entirety. The length and nature of the oration or speech itself will frequently help to determine your choice of method.

25 *Projection of Thought*

When an interpretative reader appears before any group of listeners, his purpose should be to stimulate and entertain them, rather than to display his artistic skill as a reader. He reads to them for their interest and enjoyment; they have not come to watch him perform. It is this basic purpose that determines what the reader reads and how he reads it.

Know Your Selection—When you speak your own thoughts, they have meaning to you and you speak them meaningfully. When you read aloud, you must understand and appreciate the thoughts of the author in order to read them meaningfully.

To fully understand what you are reading, you must know and appreciate the theme of the selection as a whole and its essential background factors. You must know the meaning of each paragraph, sentence, and phrase and its significance in the development of the theme. You must know the setting and its implications in the development of the theme and the action involved. You must know the characters included, their distinguishing characteristics, and their place and importance in the development of the theme. And you should know important facts about the author and the special circumstances surrounding the writing of the selection.

Use Basic Speech Skills—The effective reader evidences a thorough understanding of his material as he reads by proper phrasing of the words and the use of pauses and emphasis. Changes in pitch, intensity, duration, and quality are in harmony with the thought being expressed and aid its expression.

Phrasing, Pausing, Emphasis—By *phrasing* we mean the grouping of the words in a sentence into subsidiary groups or thought units, according to the thought being communicated, through the use of *pauses,* short and long. The pauses may or may not coincide with the grammatical punctuation within the sentence. However, the words must be appropriately grouped, for entire meanings can be changed by careless phrasing. The length of each pause will vary with the effect desired. Frequently, a pause will give emphasis to a particular word or group of words. If you pause just before the important word, you direct attention to what follows —you "point it up." Comedians frequently use this device, pausing just before the key word of the phrase and again after it to give the audience time to chuckle or laugh. Whole phrases or words within phrases which carry the more significant, special, key meanings sometimes need more accent, stress, or force than others in order that they may be *emphasized* and brought especially to the listener's attention. You must carefully determine what words or phrases should be given this special emphasis, since misplaced emphasis may distort the author's meaning.

Develop Voice Flexibility—Speakers who have flexible voices project thought more effectively while reading aloud than do those whose voices are less flexible. A flexible voice is able to respond more readily to variations and subtleties in the author's thoughts. You should practice constantly to develop a flexible voice capable of making fine as well as broad changes in pitch, intensity, and duration in order that you may project the meanings of the author's thought completely. Generally speaking, the more flexible your voice, the more effective you will be in projection of thought.

Develop Bodily Control—Selected bodily action can enrich the reader's expression of the author's thought. Work to develop control of your bodily activity in order to improve your effectiveness in projection of thought while reading aloud.

Projection of Thought Basic to Projection of Emotion—Although the projection of thought and the projection of emotion occur simultaneously, for purposes of study and practice they can be separated. Although we believe that most students need more instruction in projection of emotion than in projection of thought, let us emphasize that effectiveness in projection of thought is an essential.

26 Projection of Emotion

An author uses words not only to express thoughts, but also to express moods, feelings, and emotions. Hence, to present the author's meanings effectively, the reader must interpret not only the thoughts involved, but the moods, feelings, and emotions as well. To speak of moods, feelings, and emotions is to speak of one and the same thing, except that moods are perhaps more general than feelings. Emotions may be thought of as very intense feelings. For example, the mood of the story or the poem or the scene may be somber, heavy, or tragic; the feeling of the character involved may initially be one of utter dismay and confusion which, as it becomes more intense, may be recognized as the emotion of fear.

Causes of Inadequate Projection of Emotion—The projection of the emotional content of what the author has written is based upon how effectively the speaker projects the thought the author is expressing. That the reader must pay special attention to the projection of the emotional elements in a selection is emphasized by the fact that many who read aloud, even many with training, usually project the thought of the selection adequately, but do not project with similar effectiveness the moods, feelings, and emotions that are inherent in or accompany the thought being expressed. When the emotional elements are not expressed satisfactorily, the reader may not sense, recognize, or identify the mood, feeling, or emotion involved. Or he may not have experienced the mood, feeling, or emotion in reality or even imaginatively; hence his body or voice may have no basis for recreating its characteristics. In other words, the material he is reading may be too difficult for him. It may be beyond his emotional understanding.

The reader's body and voice may not be sufficiently flexible to create the characteristics of the mood, feeling, or emotion even though he senses it and appreciates it somewhat. Or, through lack of experience in public speaking and in interpretative reading especially, he may not be aware of what his body and voice can do in the expression of the emotional content of a selection or to what extent he must "let them go" in its expression. Or it may be that he is inhibited in speaking and especially in reading which requires emotional interpretation, because of poor adjustment in the speaking situation or because of attitudes on his part which make him react negatively to emotional expression—he "holds back" the expression of emotion rather than "giving out" as he speaks.

Characteristics of Skill in Projection of Emotion—It is clear that when we are uninhibited and speak our own thoughts, we express the related moods, feelings, and emotions appropriately and well. But it is quite different for most of us when we read aloud to listeners the thoughts of another. To present effectively what an author has written, we must speak as if what we are reading is our very own composition. It is clear that the most difficult of all is the interpretation of the emotional elements. This needed skill in projection of emotion generally and in any given selection can be developed.

The characteristics of the reader skilled in projection of emotion, which clearly indicate the goals toward which the inexperienced reader must work, are as follows:

1. He identifies, or senses readily, the moods, feelings, and emotions involved in the material he plans to read or is reading.

2. He has an appreciation for and an understanding of moods, feelings, and emotions generally and knows their nature and characteristics as a basis for producing them as he speaks. He has gained this knowledge through observation, study, and his own emotional experiences, both real and imaginary.

3. He has a readiness to interpret moods, feelings, and emotions as he reads. This readiness has been acquired through uninhibited as well as controlled experiences in reading aloud all kinds of material. He approaches what he reads with an intense inner enthusiasm and vigor.

   We recommend that the inexperienced reader begin with very simple material, such as the simpler, somewhat raucous children's stories, increasing the complexity and difficulty of the material he reads as his skill in projection of emotion increases. The children's stories may be read at sight, at first, with complete abandon and freedom of expression, the moods, feelings, and emotions being expressed as the reader reacts to them at the moment and with much exaggeration. It is best to read many stories of all kinds, stories in verse and in prose, stories that are real, fanciful, descriptive, expository, dramatic, humorous, ludicrous, glamorous, gentle, villainous, and so forth, rather than to practice a great deal on just one or two kinds. Later, some favorites may be studied and rehearsed with profit.

4. He has developed a flexible body and voice which can create the essential characteristics of the various moods, feelings, and emotions. This flexibility of body and voice can be attained best through first reading simple material with complete abandon and with exaggeration of the bodily and vocal expression that is spontaneous as the speaker reads. More difficult material should follow as the student develops flexibility of body and voice; suggestion and criticism should be increased and be made more specific as rapidly as the student can benefit from it.

This "flexibility of body and voice" is acquired as part of the "readiness to interpret" described in Point 3 above, but each may receive separate emphasis as necessary. Emphasis on one also may hasten the development of the other.

5. He knows when his body and voice are producing the necessary characteristics of the mood, feeling, or emotion to insure recognition by the audience and the response from them he desires. The reader not only knows the effect he wishes to produce in the listener, but also knows *how* to produce it and knows *when* he is producing it.

6. He has so thoroughly mastered, through study and practice, the interpretation of the author's thought and feeling, that, as he reads, his body and voice interpret from phrase to phrase instantaneously, naturally, and effortlessly what the author is saying without seeming to have studied and rehearsed that interpretation.

Learning to Express a Mood, Feeling, or Emotion—Occasionally, the reader finds it necessary to express a mood, feeling, or emotion that is not within his experience and, hence, is difficult for him to create. In such a case, we suggest that the reader attempt to induce the mood, feeling, or emotion within himself and then experiment with speaking the author's thoughts in his (the reader's) own words until his expression is convincing. Then, in the same emotional manner, he should speak these thoughts in the author's exact words and rehearse their expression until he can reproduce the author's emotional meanings at will. Although the speaker may not actually be experiencing the mood, feeling, or emotion that he is expressing, the listener responds appropriately to what the author is saying as if he were experiencing it.

Various methods are used to induce moods, feelings, or emotions within a reader. All of the following suggestions may be helpful to the student:

1. The reader relaxes his entire body and puts out of his mind all thoughts except those pertaining to what the author has written. He may sit or stand or move about slowly, as he wishes.

2. He tries to imagine, to see in his "mind's eye," the situation the author has described—the setting, the characters, and what is happening. He tries to sense through smell, taste, touch, sight, and hearing, as well as in his muscles, the nature of the surrounding atmosphere. In this imaginative condition, he may do one or a number of things to further induce within himself the appropriate emotional state:

   a. He may literally think himself into the predominant mood, feeling, or emotion he must express.
   b. He may talk himself into it.
   c. He may have someone talk him into it.

    d. He may surround himself with pictures of a similar situation portraying a similar atmosphere.

    e. He may read a story involving identical moods, feelings, or emotions or he may have an experienced performer read such a story to him.

    f. He may listen to appropriate emotional music.

3. To aid this imaginative approach, he may assume the body posture and tensions which seem most characteristic of the mood, feeling, or emotion involved and actually express it in pantomime. These assumed bodily postures, tensions, and movements may help materially in providing the muscular basis for the vocal expression of the mood, feeling, or emotion.

4. As the mood, feeling, or emotion seems to take hold of him, he may first express what he feels through noises, cries, moans, sighs, sobs, gasps, ejaculations, and so forth, followed by expression in his own words, in the same emotional manner, of what the author has written, followed by expression of the author's emotional meanings in the author's exact words.

5. He should analyze and describe what he does as he expresses the mood, feeling, or emotion to make certain that his rendition approaches reality, that it is consistent with human nature and human behavior.

6. He should repeat a number of times the emotional interpretation he has learned, using other materials in order to insure that his body and voice will have a readiness to respond appropriately when confronted with a similar mood, feeling, or emotion in his reading.

27 *Control of Bodily Activity*

    Bodily activity normally accompanies the thoughts and feelings a speaker experiences while he is speaking. As the thoughts and feelings of the author are expressed by the interpretative reader, his overall bodily movements, his arm and hand gestures, and his head movements and facial expressions may play an especially appropriate and important part in his interpretation.

    Further, the amount and kind of bodily activity used by the interpretative reader will vary with the individual reader, his selection, the occasion, and the nature of his audience, just as in speech making. Obviously, the bodily activity that a reader would use in presenting Hamlet's "Advice to the Players" speech would be greater than and of a type different from what he would use if he were reading a quiet lyric. Hence, the control of bodily activity while reading is most important.

It should be emphasized that the effective reader gives the impression of poise, naturalness, ease, and simplicity. The bodily action used in any selection should be carefully planned and rehearsed, but rehearsed sufficiently to become natural.

The basic principle of control of bodily activity in interpretative reading is that the reader suggests bodily tensions and actions rather than attempting to make them complete and real. He suggests the bodily movements of the characters he is presenting rather than attempting to act them out completely. For example, in reading of the desperate struggle of the climbers in James Ramsey Ullman's *The White Mountain,* the reader's movements would not actually be the same as those of the climbers, but rather would suggest the muscular tensions involved.

Your teacher will observe your good and bad qualities with respect to control of bodily activity while reading and will be most concerned about whether your posture is good and whether you appear well poised, handle your book properly, and have sufficient eye contact with your audience. He will be further concerned about whether your general bodily tensions and movements are appropriate, whether your specific hand and arm gestures are right and natural and your facial expressions suitable, whether the actions of the characters you are presenting are satisfactorily suggested, and whether you have any distracting bodily mannerisms.

Handling a Book or Manuscript While Reading Aloud—Except in very informal situations, most interpretative readers stand rather than sit while reading. If a reading stand or lectern is available, place your book on it; both hands are thus left free. If necessary because of your height and vision and if it is possible, adjust its height beforehand so that it will be comfortable for you. If you sit while reading, you may wish to place your book on a table of appropriate height. If you read from several sources, plan how and where you are going to place your books or papers on the reading stand or table before you read from them and as you are through with them.

If the reading stand or table cannot be adjusted to the proper height for you to be comfortable, hold your book. If you hold it, place the book in one hand, so that you will have the other free for gesturing and turning the pages. If the book is unusually large or heavy, you may need to hold it with both hands. Practice using it so that you can do so easily and so that it will not inhibit your bodily activity.

Sometimes you will read selections from different parts of a book, or you will have to cut the selection so that you need to skip many pages at a time. Some persons insert at the proper places small pieces of paper on which the page number is written, so that they know the order in which the parts follow each other; the difficulty here is that the paper slips may fall out of the book. Other readers use paper clips or rubber bands to advantage in marking the pages from which they wish to read. Some prefer to type a copy of the cutting and place it in a small looseleaf notebook, rather than read from the marked cutting. In typing the copy from which you will read, do it in double or triple space; experiment to find which method you like best.

Turn the pages quietly without attracting attention. Do not wet your finger before turning the page. As you turn the page, look ahead in order to be certain of what comes next so that there will be no break in your reading and so your performance will progress as smoothly as it would in the middle of a page.

Bodily Activity and Type of Material—The bodily activity of the speaker arises from his ideas and feelings as he expresses them. The bodily activity of the reader is directly related to the thought and emotional content of the material he is reading.

When he reads factual material for the sole purpose of presenting the ideas of the writer clearly, the bodily activity that he uses is natural and at a minimum. His posture, his general bodily attitude, his facial expressions, and his arm and hand gestures are his own; that is, they are as they would be if the ideas he is speaking were original with him at the moment.

Descriptive material may occasion more action which supplements and actually aids the reader in making the writer's ideas vivid. This action is natural also. But when, in order to read his material effectively, the reader must suggest the attitudes, feelings, emotions, and moods that the characters involved are experiencing, as well as their physical characteristics, he assumes postures, creates bodily tensions, magnifies facial expressions, and uses selected head movements and appropriate arm and hand gestures, all of which supplement his vocal expression of the author's thoughts.

What Bodily Activity to Use—Where the words are insufficient for the reader to express the writer's full meaning or where the reader's interpretation demands special emphasis, controlled bodily action should be used. But what action should be used and how? It is not possible to say here, since the material, the characteristics of the reader, and the intonation must all be considered. These questions can be answered only by saying that the reader must:

1. Develop a flexible, responsive bodily mechanism.
2. Understand and appreciate thoroughly the emotional content of his material.
3. Be observant of the behavior and reactions of people.
4. While rehearsing his reading, use his imagination to the full in experimenting with bodily action until he discovers what action best supplements the thoughts and feelings he is expressing.

5. Select the most suitable action and exaggerate it sufficiently to make certain of the listener's response to it.

Reading Recitals—Occasionally audiences gather to hear students as well as professional readers present what are frequently called "reading recitals." In such situations, the response of the audience may be influenced by a number of things that the reader can control.

The reader should consider the way the platform is "set," the lighting, his introduction (if there is a chairman), the seating of latecomers while he is reading, and so forth.

He must give special consideration to his dress and appearance. In general, simplicity in dress is best, that which is in keeping with what constitutes good grooming in any social situation. Your clothing should be in good taste for you in the specific situation from the standpoints of color, design, and fit. Your dress should not be extreme or gaudy and should never call attention to itself.

Whether formal or informal attire—a dinner dress or tuxedo or street clothes—is to be worn will be determined by the customs of the community and the nature of the occasion. Where several readers appear on the same program, it should be understood that all are to dress formally or informally—as agreed upon.

New clothes and new shoes should be worn during rehearsals so that you may acquire ease and comfort in wearing them. If you are uncomfortable in your clothes, your audience will suffer with you.

Ordinarily, no special makeup is necessary; if the lighting requires it, it may be worn, but it should not be extreme. Girls should not experiment with a new or unfamiliar arrangement of their hair.

In general, jewelry should not be worn, especially bright, reflecting ornaments and the dangling variety of bracelets and earrings.

28   Rhythm

There is rhythm in many things, for example, in the sound of the wind and the rain, marching feet, a dance, the tick of a clock, the song of a bird, the beat of a heart, the laughter of a child, the beat of a horse's hoofs, the roar of an engine, the breathing of a tired man, the chant of a crowd, the way a foreigner speaks, the way you speak naturally, and the way you speak as you express various feelings, moods, and emotions. The effective interpretative reader captures this beat, accent, and movement and controls it as he expresses the writer's thought and feeling.

Nursery rhymes when read aloud have a rhythmic sound, each according to the way it is written. In fact, all writing when read aloud has a rhythm which arises from the thought of the author and from the action, mood, emotion, and feeling he is expressing, as well as from the style of writing. In some writings, the rhyme scheme (the agreement in sounds at the ends of lines or within lines, word groupings, or repetitions) is so basic and so predominant that the reader finds it difficult to subordinate the rhythm to the thought as he reads. Ordinarily, the rhythm of the selection as such is secondary to the expression of the author's thought and feeling but arises from it.

In other words, the interpretative reader must sense the rhythm, the movement, of what he is reading—fast or slow, accented or smooth—arising out of its meaning, background, thought, and emotional content, whether description, narration, or dialogue. The thought, the mood, and the form of the writing all will help the reader to determine and control the rhythm of his expression. He must, however, avoid following the form of writing alone, lest the reading become patterned or singsong; the thought element must predominate, not the rhyme or the printed line. He must read the ideas according to their meaning as they are related to the mood and emotion being expressed, even ignoring punctuation if necessary.

29   *Pronunciation*

The interpretative reader must pay special attention to his pronunciation. Since the language used is the author's rather than the speaker's, pronunciation may be difficult. The selection may include unfamiliar words whose pronunciation must be checked in the dictionary. It may involve dialectal pronunciations whose nature may require considerable study and practice for the reader to reproduce them. The style of writing may introduce pronunciation difficulties requiring concentrated practice. It is clear that one who reads aloud to any extent must develop a range of pronunciation skills to aid him in interpreting what the author has written.

To acquire the range of pronunciation skills, one must:

1. Make a habit of looking up the pronunciation of all unfamiliar words and practicing their pronunciation sufficiently, both singly and in context, to insure natural pronunciation.
2. Train his ear to recognize pronunciation differences, such as omission, substitution, and distortion of sounds, differences in syllabification, accent, and inflection, and differences in style or manner of pronunciation, such as casual, pedantic, and the like.

3. Practice to reproduce variations in pronunciation characteristic of the various regions of the United States and the more common foreign pronunciations of English, such as Italian, Scandinavian, French, and so forth.

Effectiveness in pronunciation in interpretative reading is determined by:

1. Whether the reader can be understood both in his normal pronunciations and in his use of dialects. Too exact reproduction of a dialect may make it difficult or impossible for the listener to understand what is said. It is best to suggest only the flavor of the dialect by reproducing its outstanding and identifying characteristics.
2. Whether the style of pronunciation or the dialect used is appropriate to the author's thought and feeling; whether it helps in its interpretation and is therefore convincing.
3. Whether the pronunciation is easy, effortless, fluent, and natural. The reader's pronunciation should not call attention to itself, but rather should seem to be inherent in his interpretation. It should be emphasized that lack of fluency and ease in pronunciation may spoil the effect of the reader's interpretation.

Here is an exercise in using dictionaries to learn the pronunciation of unfamiliar words that you might encounter in the selections you choose to read aloud. These particular words are not likely to appear in your selections. In fact, they are all uncommon words, which have helped to determine the winners of the National Spelling Bee in recent years. The purpose of the exercise is to help you learn to use a dictionary as a pronunciation guide. You will need three different dictionaries to do the exercise. Try to use dictionaries from three different publishers, in order to become acquainted with the diacritical markings used by different companies.

EXERCISE IN USING PRONUNCIATION GUIDES

Select a word from this list:

1. abbacy	11. exacerbate	21. larghetto	31. scrivener
2. abrogate	12. febrile	22. manumit	32. sequitur
3. afflatus	13. flocculent	23. minatory	33. sericeous
4. asceticism	14. fuliginous	24. obloquy	34. sycophant
5. canonical	15. geophagy	25. peripatetic	35. syzygy
6. cinnabar	16. gneiss	26. peroration	36. tenebrous
7. dilettante	17. herbaceous	27. propitiatory	37. turgescence
8. edelweiss	18. homiletic	28. sacrilegious	38. ustulation
9. efflorescence	19. insouciant	29. saponaceous	39. vitiate
10. emendation	20. jocose	30. satiate	40. whorl

Write your word here _____

Write International Phonetic Symbols for the word here _____
 (**Note:** The best source of phonetic symbols is *A Pronouncing Dictionary of American English,* by Kenyon and Knott, published by the G. & C. Merriam Company. Many of these words do not appear in that volume. Many will not be found in brief paperback editions of dictionaries. When you find it, note the table near the front of the book which gives phonetic symbols for the diacritical markings used in the dictionary. Your task now becomes one of transcribing the diacritical markings into phonetics.)

What three dictionaries are you using?
 1. Name _____ Publisher _____
 2. Name _____ Publisher _____
 3. Name _____ Publisher _____

Give the complete pronunciation directions and the key to pertinent symbols for each of your dictionaries:
 (**Note:** The pronunciation directions will be printed in parentheses, immediately following the alphabetical listing of the word in the dictionary. The key to the symbols is usually at the bottom of the page. You will be interested mainly in the vowel sounds.)

 Dictionary No. 1
  Pronunciation directions:

  Key to pertinent symbols:

 Dictionary No. 2
  Pronunciation directions:

Key to pertinent symbols:

Dictionary No. 3
Pronunciation directions:

Key to pertinent symbols:

Give the derivation of the word from dictionary No. ____
Give the meaning of the word from dictionary No. ____

30   *Voice Control*

Wide Range of Voice Skills Essential—The control of the voice is a major factor in the effectiveness of the interpretative reader. Through skill in its control he secures responses from his listeners that otherwise might not be attained. Although he may cause his whole self to vibrate with the thought and feeling he is expressing, the effect of his interpretation on his listeners will depend upon the degree to which his voice is controlled to stimulate them to a complete realization of all of the essential details of that thought and feeling. Hence, the interpretative reader must have a wide range of voice skills instantaneously at his command—skills in control of pitch, intensity, duration, and quality, individually and in combination. These skills, acquired consciously at first, will become habitual with practice.

Bad Habits in Voice Control While Reading—When performances in extemporaneous speaking and reading aloud by the same persons are compared, it has been observed that many of the reading performances are characterized by one or more of the following:

1. A higher pitch level is used.
2. A more rapid rate of speaking is used.
3. The reading tends to sound monotonous—there is less variation in one or more of the attributes of voice, especially pitch, duration, and quality.
4. One or more vocal patterns, especially of pitch, intensity, and duration, are apparent.

When one (or more) of these characteristics appears, voice control is inadequate.

Steps in Developing Voice Skills—To develop the necessary range of voice skills required for effective interpretative reading, the inadequacies listed above must be eliminated. Here are some recommended steps:

1. Learn to take your time while reading and to avoid what may be called reading too rapidly. Rapid reading is not conducive to effective interpretation, whereas a slower reading rate may make it possible.
2. Learn to read in your normal pitch range, which is more nearly that used when you are speaking extemporaneously at ease and with poise.
3. Break yourself of any habits you may have of reading in patterns regardless of the author's thought and feeling. Practice to acquire a wider range in the use of pitch, intensity, duration, and quality.
4. Strive through practice to secure greater skill in the variation of pitch, intensity, duration, and quality within words, syllables, and even in sounds, as well as in phrases and sentences.

Most students will find that successful practice in these steps tends to eliminate their bad habits in voice control while reading aloud, as well as to provide the basis for acquiring a wider range of voice skills and hence greater effectiveness in interpretative reading generally.

Voice Control Should Be Spontaneous—The listener should not be aware of your voice or your control of it. He should react to the thoughts and feelings of the author, not to your voice skills as such. But, nevertheless, it is your skill in controlling your vocal instrument spontaneously and effortlessly that is the primary factor in producing a spontaneous, absorbing response from the listener. It is to be expected that the finest actors are those who are most skillful in the control of their voices.

VI ASSIGNMENTS

There are seven sets of assignments in this text:

1. Speech inventory assignments
2. Assignments on the essential skills of speech making
3. Assignments on the essential skills of reading aloud
4. Assignments related to the cultural context of speech
5. Assignments related to a field or profession
6. Assignments on incidental speaking
7. Assignments on the long speech and the long oral reading

For each assignment there are instructions on preparation, directions on delivery, and a rating blank.

The instructions on preparation include many of the things people prepare in their work: outlines, note cards, speaker's notes, manuscripts, and visual aids. Not all will be called for in the same speech. The challenge is to follow instructions. The benefit comes from practicing many or all of these preparational devices.

The directions on delivery include instructions to read from manuscript, speak from notes, hold note cards in hand, speak from the side of the speaker's stand, speak from in front of it, use a lectern, hold book in hand, and so on. Not all come in the same speech. Again, the challenge is to follow instructions. The benefit comes from practicing many different manners of delivery.

Each assignment has a rating blank. Most are specifically designed for the assignment being presented. This helps the student in his preparation since he knows that he will be rewarded for following instructions. It helps the evaluator because he has no extraneous criteria to disregard or try to adapt. It reduces the amount of critical comments he has to write.

It is understood by experienced teachers that in a class of twenty it is hard to have each student give more than seven or eight speeches during a term, what with text reviews, lectures by the instructor, examinations, thorough explanations of assignments, and whatever else takes up class time. The purpose of the many assignments is two-fold: to give an instructor and class a series of options in choosing assignments to fit the needs of the group; and to provide for different courses, in which the identity of the group may be either interest- or occupation-oriented. For example, the diagnostic assignments may be used by any group, whether beginners or advanced. The assignments on the essential skills of speech making serve very well for a beginning class in speech. The sets on reading aloud would be useful for a beginning speech class or for a beginning course in interpretation. The sets related to the cultural context and to a field or profession are most appropriate for a course in business and professional speaking. The sections on the long speech and the long oral reading are most serviceable for a second course in speech making, or interpretation.

Much that an instructor might wish to use as lecture material is available in the dozens of excellent general speech texts. Any of them could be assigned as collateral reading. These assignments are designed to help students in their preparation and presentation of speeches.

31   Speech Inventory Assignments

There are six assignments in this section. Your instructor will decide how many he wishes to use with your class. Some instructors may use them all. Others may feel that two or three are sufficient to show "where you are now" in your progress toward becoming an effective speaker.

ASSIGNMENT A-1

Please write down a good bit of information about yourself, according to the following suggestions. Prepare to hand the paper in for your instructor to see. Then plan to stop at his office to discuss your background with him. Organize your material according to these eight items:

1. *Personal:* Include your name, age, birthplace, present address, and phone number. How is your health? Have you ever had any serious illness?
2. *Education:* Include grade school, high school, college, present status in school, and major interests in school.
3. *Family:* How many in your family? Are your parents living? Where were your father and mother born? What language was spoken in their home? What language do they speak now? Who taught you to

speak? With whom do you live now? What is the occupation of your parents?

4. *Travel:* In what towns and cities have you lived and at what ages? To what states and countries have you traveled? Are you able to speak any language other than English?

5. *Work:* Have you worked part-time or full-time anywhere? Doing what? What do you want to make your life's work?

6. *Hobbies and Activities:* What do you like to do in your leisure time? Name the magazines you read regularly. Name the last three books you have read. Do you take part in civic, fraternal, or church activities? What?

7. *Speaking:* Have you had opportunity to speak to groups within the past year? What was the occasion? Within the past five years? On what occasions? Have you had any previous courses in speech? Have you had private lessons in interpretation or dramatics? Do the members of your family do public speaking? How do you feel when you are asked to make a talk? Have you ever been in a play or speech contest?

8. *Self-evaluation:* Think of several people whom you consider good speakers. In what characteristics are you like them? That is, what assets do you have that might make you a good speaker? Do you have some characteristics that might hinder your becoming a good speaker—some liabilities, so to speak?

ASSIGNMENT A-2

Now, let us give you a chance to make a short speech in order to estimate your adequacy in the basic behaviors of speech. Select one statement from among those listed below, to be used as the subject of your speech. You may explain it, interpret its meaning, or discuss its significance. Illustrate it with examples from your own experience if possible. Do not write out this little talk. You probably won't even need an outline. Plan your talk by thinking about it. Do not memorize it word for word. Plan to talk for not less than two nor more than three minutes. Present the talk extemporaneously and without notes when you are called on. Give your handbook to your instructor. He will evaluate your presentation by marking each of the four items in the appropriate column. Most people are adequate in these four aspects. Accordingly, most of the scores will be "4." Some may be good, "5." A few may be very good, "6." There may even be a student now and then who will be superior, "7." On the other hand, some may be poor, or very poor, or inferior, in which event the instructor will check the column for "3," "2," or "1." In that case he will underline the explanatory words that indicate in what way he is not adequate.

Each of the following statements is the last sentence of one of Aesop's fables.

The race is not always to the swift.
It is very foolish to be greedy.
Do not believe everything that you hear.
Pride goes before a fall.
Might makes right.
Learn from the misfortunes of others.
Friends in fine weather only are not worth much.
A kindness is never wasted.
If you try to please all you please none.
Self help is the best help.
Ability proves itself by deeds.
Misfortune is the test of true friendship.
Whatever you do, do with all your might.
There is nothing worth so much as liberty.
A possession is worth no more than the use we make of it.
Wicked deeds will not stay hid.
Do not count your chickens before they are hatched.
Take warning from the misfortunes of others.
An act of kindness is well repaid.
Be content with your lot.
Honesty is the best policy.
In unity is strength.
Act in haste and repent at leisure.
Look before you leap.
Do not grudge others what you cannot enjoy yourself.
Greatness has its penalties.
Take what you can get when you can get it.
One falsehood leads to another.
Stick to your trade.
However unfortunate we may think we are, there is always someone worse off than ourselves.
Do not play tricks on your neighbors unless you can stand the same treatment yourself.
Be sure you can better your condition before you seek a change.
There's a time for work and a time for play.
Deeds count, not boasting words.
Precious things are without value to those who cannot prize them.
You are judged by the company you keep.
It is easy to be brave when there is no danger.
Heaven helps those who help themselves.
Do not let anything turn you from your purpose.

Note: Some instructors have found that they can evaluate your adequacy in these basic behaviors of speech if you use some other type of introductory "ice-breaker" or "get-acquainted" speech. You and your instructor may decide to do this. Go ahead. It serves the same purpose. But don't talk too long.

A-2 EVALUATION   The Basic Behaviors of Speech
(An individual diagnosis)

Date _____   Student _____

Subject _____

| Adjustment to the Speaking Situation: | 7 6 5 4 3 2 1 |

Inadequacies: Ill at ease; unnatural; tense; inhibited; nervous; excited; frightened; hesitant; uncertain; chaotic; bodily mannerisms; unable to speak coherently, fluently, emphatically.

| Formulation of Thought: | 7 6 5 4 3 2 1 |

Inadequacies: *Successive thoughts* unrelated, interrupted, inconsistent; *Statements* ambiguous, obscure, inexact, incomplete, frequent grammatical errors; *Vocabulary* limited, inaccurate, colloquial, dull, inexpressive; *Pronunciation* distracting.

| Articulation: | 7 6 5 4 3 2 1 |

Inadequacies: Organic abnormality; jerky, uneven utterance; incorrect formation of some speech sounds; inaccurate formation of speech sounds; inactivity of the articulators; rapid rate of utterance; foreign accent. Needs further analysis.

| Phonation: | 7 6 5 4 3 2 1 |

Inadequacies: Organic abnormality; *Pitch* too high, upward slide, falling inflection; *Intensity* too weak, too loud; *Duration*—tones held for too short a time, too long a time; *Quality*—improper balance or control of resonance, unpleasant, peculiar; voice lacks flexibility. Needs further analysis.

COMMENTS:

ASSIGNMENT A-3

The third step in our inventory is designed to give us an idea of your present ability in the essential skills of speech making. To do this we ask you to make the best speech you possibly can to your classmates. You may speak on any subject you wish. You may give an informative speech, an argumentative speech, or an entertaining speech. You may talk about persons, places, things, events, experiences, opinions, or any other thing.

This speech should be three minutes in length—no more, no less. It is important for you to be able to stay within time limits. Remember that there are other speakers to be heard.

112

Plan your speech well. You should have several days to prepare after the assignment has been made. Begin early. Choose a subject for your speech that is worth talking about, that encompasses material worth listening to, and that arises out of a background with which you are familiar. Do not use a speech you have previously given.

Analyze the subject and carefully select the points you wish to present. Sort your material so that it is definitely related to your subject and the specific points you wish to develop. Arrange the material to secure unity, coherence, and emphasis.

Write out a detailed outline of the speech. This outline is to be handed to your instructor together with your handbook before you go to the platform to speak. Study the outline so that you are thoroughly familiar with the order in which you wish to present your material. Do not memorize the speech word for word. Practice the speech aloud many times.

When you are called upon, go to the platform and speak loudly enough to be heard; speak clearly and distinctly; speak to secure the attention and interest of the audience; speak with vigor and enthusiasm.

This speech is important; it is essential that you be at your best. You may not speak as well or you may speak more effectively than others. In either case be sure that this performance is the best you can do.

A-3 EVALUATION   *Essential Skills of Speech Making*

Date _____   Student _____

Subject _____

Choice of Subject	7	6	5	4	3	2	1	*COMMENTS:*
Choice of Thought	7	6	5	4	3	2	1	
Choice of Material	7	6	5	4	3	2	1	
Organization of Material	7	6	5	4	3	2	1	
Use of Language	7	6	5	4	3	2	1	
Projection to the Audience	7	6	5	4	3	2	1	
Control of Bodily Activity	7	6	5	4	3	2	1	
Rhythm	7	6	5	4	3	2	1	
Pronunciation	7	6	5	4	3	2	1	
Voice Control	7	6	5	4	3	2	1	

ASSIGNMENT A-4

The next step in this inventory gives us information about your ability in the essential skills of reading aloud.

Choose a poem or poems (limit your performance to two minutes in length) that you like. Study your material until you are thoroughly familiar with the thought and feeling expressed by the author. Practice reading it aloud many times, until you are sure you are expressing the thought and feeling of the author in a way that may be appreciated by the audience.

When you are called upon, go to the platform and read so that you can be heard; read clearly and distinctly, in a vivid, stimulating manner; read to the audience, not to yourself; read in a natural style; do not be artificial. A certain thrill comes to both speaker and audience from good literature vividly interpreted.

Begin your performance with brief introductory remarks. You may comment upon the author, the poem, why you like it, and what it means to you. Read your selection from the printed page so that the audience may fully appreciate the thought which the author has to express. You must do more than merely read aloud. You must interpret, simply but effectively, the thought and feeling of the author.

Again, this is an important assignment. Do your best. You should work at it for several days ahead of your performance. Give your handbook to your instructor before you read so that he may record his impressions of your reading.

Note: There are some paragraphs of prose from orations, essays, and so forth, which would serve very well for this asignment. Check with your instructor as to which would be better for you.

A-4 EVALUATION   *Achievement in Reading Aloud*

Date _____   Student _____

Selection _____   Author _____

Choice of Material	7 6 5 4 3 2 1	*COMMENTS:*
Arrangement of Material	7 6 5 4 3 2 1	
Projection of Thought	7 6 5 4 3 2 1	
Projection of Emotion	7 6 5 4 3 2 1	
Control of Bodily Activity	7 6 5 4 3 2 1	
Rhythm	7 6 5 4 3 2 1	
Pronunciation	7 6 5 4 3 2 1	
Voice Control	7 6 5 4 3 2 1	

ASSIGNMENT A-5

We have already noted your voice as you produced it in the assignment on the basic processes. Most people have adequate phonation, but it won't take long to make another analysis, this time checking items which you might work on.

Read aloud the following diagnostic passage for voice and connected speech. All of the sounds used in English speech are included in the first paragraph and repeated later. Practice reading the passage several times so that you may read it as naturally as possible. It is factual, unemotional prose material. As you read it, your evaluator can concentrate on the pitch, rate, volume, and quality of your voice production. On the day appointed, give your handbook to your instructor as you go to the front of the room to read. Read from a distance of about twenty feet.

The Astrodome

As the fans gathered in their orange, azure, or blue seats in the ballpark to watch the Colt 45s, they became more and more intrigued with the construction nearby. The size of the excavation suggested that the building would be huge. When the hole in the earth filled with water it

A-5 EVALUATION   Phonation
(A more detailed diagnosis)

Evaluation

		Inadequacies	Faulty	Severe
Quality	7 6 5 4 3 2 1	Quality		
Pitch	7 6 5 4 3 2 1	Muffled		
Duration	7 6 5 4 3 2 1	Metallic		
Intensity	7 6 5 4 3 2 1	Nasal		
Flexibility	7 6 5 4 3 2 1	Denasal		
		Harsh		
		Hoarse-Husky		
		Breathy		
		Infantile		
		Pitch		
		High		
		Low		
		Inflection pattern		
		Duration		
		Staccato		
		Perseveration		
		Intensity		
		Too weak		
		Too loud		
		Organic abnormality		
		Nature of:		

COMMENTS:

Student _____

Evaluator _____   Date _____

looked like a lake. After the pumping was complete and the crater was dry enough to resume work, the walls were erected and the great round arches of the dome were swung into place by the giant cranes.

The plastic sections of the dome caused many a conjecture. Would they let the sunlight in? Would grass grow under filtered light? How much artificial illumination would be necessary?

As time went on the structure assumed its outward appearance. The perpendicular walls seemed like filigree lace. The dome itself sat there in the midst of a great open space, flanked by oil wells, easily seen for ten miles. It was called the Astrodome, the Eighth Wonder of the World, the home of the Houston Astros.

No one could anticipate the first impression the spectator gets on walking up the entrance ramp, going through the gates to the air-conditioned interior, and there seeing multicolored cushioned seats for fifty thousand people.

To be sure, there were problems. The players complained that they could not see the ball against the sky during an afternoon game. So, the transparent sections of plastic were painted blue. That brought the problem of the grass into focus. It just couldn't grow without sun and rain. So, an artificial green carpet was developed, tried out, approved, and put down.

About other ball clubs it is possible to say, "Some you win, some you lose, and some get rained out." Win? Yes. Lose? Yes. But get rained out? In the Astrodome? Never!

ASSIGNMENT A-6

We have also checked your articulation before, but we have not listened to your speech sounds with planned concentration.

Arranged below are twelve groups of sentences. Each group emphasizes a certain sound—sounds commonly misarticulated by people who have articulatory problems.

Read the sentences aloud several times before you come to class. Be sure that you can pronounce all the words. When you are called upon, read the designated paragraphs slowly, clearly, and distinctly. If you are assigned number 1, read item number 1 in each of the groups; if number 2 is assigned to you, read item number 2 in each of the groups; and so on.

Read from the front of the room. Your instructor will check the sounds he hears inaccurately made. All the groups concentrate on a consonant sound. If you make the vowel sounds in an unusual manner, he will note them as you read along through all the sentences.

It may be that your articulation will be affected by an identifiable cause. For example, there may be apparent organic deviations, such as poorly occluded teeth, cleft palate or lip, bothersome tongue, or uncontrolled facial muscles.

Your speech may be marred by faulty rhythm, such as excessive speed of utterance without variety, too much drawl, extreme hesitation, or excessive repetitions.

Perhaps your problem is having your English speech affected by a foreign language which you speak naturally.

Or perhaps you speak inaccurately as the result of carelessness, slighting of sounds, or oral inactivity.

[s]

1. In accordance with prevailing custom, the celebrated congressman closed his office and saw the opening baseball game of the season.

2. The professor was surprised at the sustained publicity which he received concerning his theories on business and finance during the banking crisis.

3. The surgeon was pessimistic concerning the recovery of the sixty-seven-year-old nurse from a severe illness.

[z]

1. President Theodore Roosevelt shook hands with each of the dignitaries from Brazil, congratulating them upon their zest and enthusiasm in so zealously espousing their cause.

2. Thousands of frenzied students zigzagged through the maze of traffic in the busy streets, cheering the team which rose to its zenith that day.

3. The zoologist who was chosen to lead the expedition to New Zealand desired to use natives as guides.

[ʌ] and [w]

1. The warden whispered to the deputy that a low whistle was to be the signal for the somewhat ill-timed jail break.

2. When the attorney asked the witness, "Why did you murder your wife?" he turned white, asked for a glass of water, then waited awhile, before whispering his answer.

3. As winter approached and the wind whistled through the trees, the occupants of the old white house were certain that their hard work during the summer had been worthwhile.

[θ]

1. As I finished reading the book, I could think of nothing else but the theories of the author regarding youth, wealth, and death.

2. Anything that the authority said about growth and health made me thankful that I had heard his theories.

3. Thirty youthful marathon runners threaded their way through the streets of the city from north to south, seeking a prize worth one thousand dollars.

[ð]

1. Although the greens were smooth, my brother had trouble with his putting. The ball would roll on either side of the cup rather than into it.

2. "When I breathe rapidly I am bothered with severe chest pains,"

my brother said. The doctor then bandaged his chest to soothe the affliction.

3. Though the weather was warm and the surface of the lake was smooth, we did breathe easier when we reached the other shore.

[ʃ] and [ʒ]

1. The official conclusion of the jury was that the sheriff did not intentionally shoot the garage owner. It was his wish to stop a foolish quarrel.

2. The passengers aboard the British liner rushed to the main deck following the crash. The prestige of the ship's captain and his sharp commands prevented confusion. Upon investigation, conditions were found not to be serious.

3. John Shorey, the County Attorney, assured the judge that he would furnish evidence shortly that would prove that the explosion in the garage that killed Parish was intentional.

[tʃ]

1. The hunters, chilled with the cold and very much dismayed, returned empty-handed. As they stretched before the fire that evening, each told of seeing a flock of baby prairie chickens just beyond the orchard, which in each case was left unmolested.

2. The new preacher spoke with unusual charm. His sermons were cherished by young and old, by rich and poor. He achieved success through simplicity of thoughts, words, and speech.

3. Word came to Coach Arthur Chambers that the Larchwood players knew his team's signals. He had one week in which to effect a change. Secret practices were charted. Several watchmen guarded the field.

[dʒ]

1. According to the legend, the gypsies sought revenge against the king because of unjust treatment. They had hoped that he would be generous as a result of their pledge.

2. The stage was set for the trial of the surgeon. The jurors were in their places. A large crowd filled the room. The judge began by objecting to the apparent prejudice of the crowd.

3. A majority of the council approved the budget. The mayor, who had made a pledge to reduce taxes, vetoed it because in his judgment the change in the salary schedule was not justified.

[t] and [d]

1. A terrible accident occurred just before dawn at the grade crossing. The Dover Limited struck a bus broadside, killed ten persons outright, and severely injured two others.

2. The statement, "United we stand, divided we fall," true at other

times in our history, is equally true today. Our present need is for leadership that definitely inspires and commands unity.

3. Recently in debate tournaments all over the land, high-school students discussed the advisability of direct Federal aid to public education.

[m], [n] and [ŋ]

1. The annual income of the nation has been less than its expenses during the last few years. The problem has been one of finding new methods of raising more money in the face of a sinking volume of business. Our leaders are thankful that business seems to be more normal this year than last.

2. Several years ago a newspaper correspondent said: "The clank of

A-6 EVALUATION   Articulation
(A more detailed diagnosis)

Date _____   Student _____

		Incorrect Speech Sounds			Other Articulation Problems		
Group	Sound	Severe	Faulty	Problem		Severe	Faulty
1	[s]			Organic			
2	[z]			Teeth			
3	[ʌ] and [w]			Lips			
4	[θ]			Tongue			
5	[ð]			Palates			
6	[ʃ] and [ʒ]			Facial muscles			
7	[tʃ]			Rhythm			
				Excessive speed			
8	[dʒ]			Excessive drawl			
9	[t] and [d]			Jerky			
10	[m], [n] and [ŋ]			Foreign accent			
11	[l]			Nationality:			
12	[r]			Oral inactivity			
Vowels	[ɛ]						
and	[ɑɪ]						
Diphthongs	[ɑʊ]						

war machinery rings anew, heralding an impending conflict. Colonial expansion, armament, aggression are the order of the day. Our national policy of neutrality may not protect us from war if it comes."

3. From roving gangs of boys in our large cities come many of our most notorious young outlaws. They commit minor crimes at first, but soon gain confidence with each successful attempt. From apprentice gangsters they become hardened criminals and enemies of the nation.

[1]

1. The new law passed by the city council failed to lower appreciably the cost of electricity to the small consumer as planned.

2. From the top of Indian Lookout Hill one saw in the valley below mile upon mile of freshly cultivated fields broken only by a lazy river winding its way toward the distant bluffs.

3. In recent years the relief of distress among the unemployed has increased local, state, and national expenditures greatly. It is said that though unemployment may be lessened its complete elimination is questioned.

[r]

1. With a roar of approval, the Harvard football team rushed onto the field. They were facing a fierce encounter with their old rivals from Princeton.

2. The reception arranged for the Byrd expedition on its return from two years of adventure in the Antarctic was a success.

3. Owing to the abnormal rains, the streams overflowed their banks and the river rose to flood stage, causing a feeling of general alarm.

32   Assignments in the Essential Skills of Speech Making

The assignments below are designed to help you develop your skill in the essential skills of speech making. They are cumulative in design, that is, each builds on what was accomplished in the preceding.

Your instructor may wish to vary the procedure from class to class by eliminating some assignments with some groups or by repeating assignments with other groups. He may wish to alternate assignments in speech making and reading aloud.

Preparing Your Speeches—You will no doubt be called upon frequently in this course to make speeches. To achieve your best you must prepare each speech carefully. It is wise to extend your preparation over a long rather than a short period of time. Think about the speech, work it over, and study it for short periods daily. Follow in order the steps listed below:

1. Choose for your speech a general subject that arises out of a background with which you are familiar.
2. Choose a central thought (a specific phase of this general subject) that can be completely developed in the time allowed. Gather material to support this central thought.
3. Divide this central thought into subordinate points in terms of the material you have gathered.
4. Plan the body of your speech. Arrange the subpoints in an order best suited for the development of your central thought. Choose and arrange the material for the development of your points.
5. Plan your conclusion.
6. Now that you know *what* you must introduce, plan your introduction.
7. Practice the speech aloud many times just as you plan to speak it to the audience.

ASSIGNMENT B-1

Aim of assignment: To learn to identify and use the four parts of a speech.

Type of performance: A talk of any type on any subject in which you have a background. *Do not talk about a trip.*

Length of performance: Not more than two minutes.

Reference material: Study "Organization of Material," Section 16, Part III of this speech handbook.

B-1 EVALUATION

Date _____   Student _____

Subject _____

Four Parts Evident								
(Organization of Material)	7	6	5	4	3	2	1	COMMENTS:
Choice of Subject	7	6	5	4	3	2	1	
Choice of Material	7	6	5	4	3	2	1	
Use of Language								
(General Evaluation)	7	6	5	4	3	2	1	
Presentation								
(Projection, Bodily Activity,								
Rhythm, Pronunciation, Voice)	7	6	5	4	3	2	1	

Specific method: Prepare the speech according to the seven steps listed in the introduction to this section.

Suggestions: Choose interesting material. Avoid worrying about the mechanics of delivery. *Make the four parts stand out clearly.*

ASSIGNMENT B-2

Aim of assignment: To learn to formulate the central thought of a speech and use it correctly.

Type of performance: A talk of any type on any subject with which you are familiar. *Do not talk about a trip,* because there is seldom a central thought when you tell what you did from day to day on a trip.

Length of performance: To be determined by the class.

Reference material: Review "Choice of Thought," Section 14, and "Organization of Material," Section 16 of this handbook.

Specific method: Prepare according to the seven steps in the introduction to this section. Write out the central thought several times, until it is phrased to suit you and according to the principles.

Repeated functions: Be sure that the speech has four parts as in Assignment B-1.

Suggestions: Choose interesting material. Avoid worrying about the mechanics of delivery, and make the four parts stand out clearly. Be sure that the central thought is stated at least three times.

B-2 EVALUATION

Date _____   Student _____

Subject _____

		COMMENTS:
Central Thought	7 6 5 4 3 2 1	
Choice of Subject	7 6 5 4 3 2 1	
Choice of Material	7 6 5 4 3 2 1	
Organization of Material	7 6 5 4 3 2 1	
Presentation (as in B-1)	7 6 5 4 3 2 1	

ASSIGNMENT B-3

Aim of assignment: To learn to divide the central thought into subpoints around which the material and details may be arranged and to state these subpoints properly.

Type of performance: A talk of any type on any subject with which you are familiar. *Do not talk about a trip.*

Length of performance: Two to four minutes.

Reference material: Review "Choice of Thought," Section 14.

Specific method: Prepare the speech according to the seven steps mentioned before. Divide your central thought into two or three points, no more. Name point one "First" and point two "Second" and so on. Refer to the points while making your speech as "First," "Second," and so forth.

Repeated functions: Be sure that your speech has four distinct parts, that the central thought conforms to the principles, and that it is stated at least three times.

Suggestions: Choose a subject that lends itself to division into two or three points. Choose interesting material. Don't worry about the mechanics of delivery. Make the four parts and especially the central thought and subpoints stand out clearly.

B-3 EVALUATION

Date _____   Student _____

Subject _____

Choice of Thought	7	6	5	4	3	2	1	*COMMENTS:*
Choice of Subject	7	6	5	4	3	2	1	
Choice of Material	7	6	5	4	3	2	1	
Organization of Material	7	6	5	4	3	2	1	
Subpoint Presentation	7	6	5	4	3	2	1	
Presentation (as in B-1)	7	6	5	4	3	2	1	

ASSIGNMENT B-4

Aim of assignment: To learn to relate and connect your material, your subpoints, and your central thought by use of the techniques of repetition, transition, and summary; also, to learn to use the blackboard.

Type of performance: Draw a diagram on the blackboard designed to give the audience a specific bit of information.

Length of performance: Not more than five minutes.

Reference material: Review items relative to the *body* of the speech under "Organization of Material," Section 16.

Specific method: Let the information you wish to give be the central thought of your speech. State it as such. Divide it into only two points, if possible. After you have developed your first point state, repeat, and summarize in one sentence what you have thus far accomplished. Example (from a speech about a football play): "In brief, deception in the *option play* is brought about by _____" (here the speaker quickly traces over the diagram the movements of players *a, b, c, d, etc.*). Your next sentence should repeat in a phrase your first point, then lead into and connect it to the second point. Example: "Now that it is clear that deception is an important aspect of the *option play,* let us consider the importance of speed in its execution." Your next sentence should repeat the general reference to speed, specifically. Example: "Speed is the second important factor in the success of the *option play.*" Repeat the above procedure after the second point has been completed and lead into the conclusion. Example: "The element of speed contributes to the success of the *option play* then, as follows: (here the speaker briefly illustrates on the diagram what he has said about speed). This factor of speed when combined with deception makes the *option play* useful in the attack of any football team. And so, when you see a team begin a play in this manner (refer to diagram), with the movement of the players in this manner (refer to diagram), with the quarterback—(etc., etc.), and the ball is carried down the field for twenty yards, you will know that deception and speed have collaborated successfully in making the *option play* an important weapon in the offensive team's attack."

Repeated functions: Your speech should have four parts—a central thought correctly stated and repeated and two subpoints correctly stated.

Suggestions: Choose an interesting subject that lends itself to picturization and that has two obvious points for which the diagram may be conveniently utilized. Do not explain something about which everybody knows.

Make the diagram large enough to be seen by all. While you are drawing it keep talking about it to the audience. Make this discussion part of the introduction. Look at the audience occasionally. Don't talk to the blackboard. Do not stand in front of the diagram when you explain it. Stand at the side. Actually use the diagram to make your points clear. Do not be afraid of repeating your explanation too often.

B-4 EVALUATION

Date _____   Student _____

Subject _____

		COMMENTS:
Use of Blackboard	7 6 5 4 3 2 1	
Transitions	7 6 5 4 3 2 1	
Conclusion	7 6 5 4 3 2 1	
Choice of Subject	7 6 5 4 3 2 1	
Choice of Thought	7 6 5 4 3 2 1	
Organization of Material	7 6 5 4 3 2 1	
Projection to Audience	7 6 5 4 3 2 1	
Bodily Activity	7 6 5 4 3 2 1	

ASSIGNMENT B-5

Aim of assignment: To learn to conclude your speech properly and to use the conclusion as an aid in emphasizing, in making your points clear, and in adapting them to the audience; further, to use the blackboard again.

Type of performance: Use the same type of speech as in Assignment

B-4. Use two sections of the blackboard this time. Diagram Point 1 on one board and Point 2 on the second. You might even separate the two sections on which you draw by a blank section between. In this way you will have to move about as you talk.

Length of performance: Not more than five minutes.

Reference material: Review items relative to the *conclusion* under "Organization of Material."

Specific method: Divide the central thought into the two points you wish to illustrate by the diagram. If you have more than two subpoints, you will need more sections of blackboard on which to draw your diagrams. After you have worked out the body of the speech, plan the conclusion to lift out and emphasize the two points which you have made. Relate these points to the central thought, showing how you have used them as definite steps in its development. Adapt and apply the point of the central thought to the audience, making it a part of their knowledge. Relate it to the activities of their everyday life. You must do more than repeat and summarize.

Repeated function: Your speech should have four parts—a correctly stated and repeated central thought and two subpoints correctly stated. You should use repetitions, transitions, and summaries as outlined in Assignment B-4.

Suggestions: Be sure that your subject is new and interesting. Watch your audience carefully during the body of the speech and determine from their reactions if your explanation is clear. If they seem to express uncertainty, do not hesitate to repeat those parts of the explanation which seem difficult. Be as brief, yet complete, as possible.

B-5 EVALUATION

Date _____   Student _____

Subject _____

		COMMENTS:
Use of Blackboard	7 6 5 4 3 2 1	
Transitions	7 6 5 4 3 2 1	
Conclusion	7 6 5 4 3 2 1	
Choice of Subject	7 6 5 4 3 2 1	
Organization of Material	7 6 5 4 3 2 1	
Projection to Audience	7 6 5 4 3 2 1	
Bodily Activity	7 6 5 4 3 2 1	

ASSIGNMENT B-6

Aim of assignment: To learn to introduce your speech properly, to make your introductory remarks serve the functions of providing a background for, arousing interest in, and leading up to the central thought of your speech.

Type of performance: Select and bring to class an object, a picture, a map, a work of art, a toy, an instrument, a tool, an appliance, or a product, which you can display to the audience. Be sure it is large enough to be seen. If it can be taken apart and put together again, so much the better. Do not use a familiar object such as a pencil or a fountain pen unless you can make an unusually interesting speech about it.

Length of performance: Not more than four minutes.

Reference material: Review items relative to the *introduction* under "Organization of Material."

Specific method: Let the information you wish to give about the object be the central thought of your speech. State it definitely. Divide it into two or three points. If you have followed the seven recommended steps in preparing your speech, the central thought, the body, and the conclusion are now planned. Obviously you need to introduce the object as well as your speech about it to the audience. Decide what historical or background material you need to give concerning it, what personal remarks you need to make about it, what you need to do to interest your audience in it, and what new terms you need to define in order to discuss it.

Arrange your material in such an order that the audience is led directly and naturally into a consideration of the central thought. Plan each step carefully and rehearse it until you can present it smoothly.

Repeated functions: Your speech should have four parts—an introduction, a carefully and correctly stated central thought, two or three well-stated points connected by transitions and emphasized by repetitions and summaries, and a conclusion which reiterates and adapts the subpoints to the central thought and the central thought to the audience.

Suggestions: Avoid simply holding the object. Display it, hold it up, walk down to the audience, or walk among them displaying it so that all may see. Manipulate it, take it apart, put it together several times, actually use it as a device for making your points clear. Do not let the audience pass the object from person to person. It distracts from your talk.

Avoid a long, trite, ordinary, pointless introduction. Begin with the familiar and work to the unfamiliar. Make your introduction serve a definite purpose, get you off to a good start, make the audience desire to hear what is to follow.

B-6 EVALUATION

Date _____   Student _____

Subject _____

Projection to Audience	7	6	5	4	3	2	1	COMMENTS:
Bodily Activity								
(Use of Object)		7	6	5	4	3	2	1
Choice of Subject		7	6	5	4	3	2	1
Thought, Material,								
Organization		7	6	5	4	3	2	1
Use of Language		7	6	5	4	3	2	1
Rhythm, Voice Control		7	6	5	4	3	2	1

ASSIGNMENT B-7

Aim of assignment: To experiment with the development of effectiveness in projection to the audience through telling a well-known story in your own words.

Type of performance: Select a child's story which you remember and which you used to like as a child, such as *Red Riding Hood, The Three Bears, The Three Little Pigs,* or *Peter Rabbit.* Be sure that there are at least two characters in the story who speak one to another. Condense the story and tell it to the audience in your own words. Endeavor to amuse them with the characters, the events, and the fun which is in the story.

Length of performance: Not more than three minutes.

Specific method: Select your story, then condense it. Plan to present only the most important details, the most important characters, and the most amusing speeches of the characters. Experiment with the voices of the different characters. Exaggerate them to communicate the exaggerated ideas of the story. Remember that these stories are sheer exaggeration and must be so treated. Make the emotional aspects of the story vivid, thrilling, and startling. Arrange the points of the story and the details of its development in climactic order.

Repeated functions: Make each word and phrase vivid. Let the audience feel your endeavor to make the story live through interpreting the richness of it. Make brief introductory remarks to the audience before you begin the story.

Suggestions: Approach your performance and your audience with a spirit of good fun. Look at them, talk to them, laugh with them, whether it be at you or the story. Watch your audience; be sure you are stimulating them the way you intend. From time to time during your preparation, read aloud from a book of children's stories to experiment with voice control.

B-7 EVALUATION

Date _____   Student _____

Story _____

Selection of Story	7	6	5	4	3	2	1	COMMENTS:
Introduction	7	6	5	4	3	2	1	
Projection to Audience	7	6	5	4	3	2	1	
Pronunciation	7	6	5	4	3	2	1	
Rhythm	7	6	5	4	3	2	1	
Voice Control	7	6	5	4	3	2	1	
Bodily Activity	7	6	5	4	3	2	1	

127

ASSIGNMENT B-8

Aim of assignment: To experiment with the development of effectiveness in projection to the audience through relating a thrilling experience of your own.

Type of performance: Select the most vivid, thrilling experience you have had, one that affected you intensely and emotionally. Relate the experience and reproduce for your audience your feelings just as you felt them.

Length of performance: Not over three minutes.

Reference material: Study "Use of Language," Section 17.

Specific method: Go over in your mind the experience as you remember it. Select those details essential to the development for the audience of the thrill you had. Arrange them in order, leading to the climax. Carefully plan each sentence from beginning to end. Choose only the most vivid and specific words. Let the emotions you felt at the time dominate your behavior as you speak. Experiment with your presentation until you are able to make it real, vivid, and startling. The audience must follow every phase of the experience with anxiety and there should be a feeling of relief on their part, when you have finished, such as you felt in the original experience. Introduce the story with brief remarks; likewise, conclude with a few brief remarks appropriate to the situation.

Repeated functions: Exaggerate sufficiently your interpretation of the experience so that the audience is aware of the depth of your feelings. Estimate the type of reaction your audience should give to the story. Plan to secure it. Try as hard as you can to define the meaning of each word and phrase for the audience through use of your voice. Look at them, talk to them, and be thrilled with them. Watch their reactions; if they do not behave as you think they should, project more intently.

Suggestions: If you have had no thrilling experience which you wish to tell, use an imaginary one or tell one of which you have heard or read. This is more difficult to do well since you have not experienced it yourself

B-8 EVALUATION

Date _____   Student _____

Experience _____

Selection of Experience	7	6	5	4	3	2	1	COMMENTS:
Introduction	7	6	5	4	3	2	1	
Projection to Audience	7	6	5	4	3	2	1	
Use of Language	7	6	5	4	3	2	1	
Pronunciation	7	6	5	4	3	2	1	
Rhythm	7	6	5	4	3	2	1	
Voice Control	7	6	5	4	3	2	1	
Bodily Activity	7	6	5	4	3	2	1	

and consequently may not be able to feel it emotionally. Strive hard for that audience response characterized as "a room so quiet you could hear a pin drop," a sigh of relief at the end, followed by applause.

ASSIGNMENT B-9

Aim of assignment: To repeat what was attempted in Assignment B-8 by use of a humorous experience.

Type of performance: Select the most embarrassing or the most humorous experience you have ever had. Tell the experience and reproduce for your audience your feelings at the time, exactly as you felt them.

Length of performance: Not more than three minutes.

Specific method: Refer to Assignment B-8 and in your preparation follow the points mentioned therein.

Repeated functions: Exaggerate your interpretation of the experience to produce a humorous effect. Make each word and phrase, as vocally expressed, define your thought and feeling. Follow your audience reaction; adapt your style to it.

Suggestions: If you have no humorous or embarrassing experience to tell about, make up one or tell one of which you have read or heard. If you do the latter you must get into the spirit of it and present it as if you had experienced it. Use every available method to build up your experience and get your audience to laugh at its humorous elements.

B-9 EVALUATION

Date _____   Student _____

Experience _____

Selection of Experience	7 6 5 4 3 2 1	*COMMENTS:*
Projection to Audience	7 6 5 4 3 2 1	
Use of Language	7 6 5 4 3 2 1	
Pronunciation	7 6 5 4 3 2 1	
Rhythm	7 6 5 4 3 2 1	
Voice Control	7 6 5 4 3 2 1	
Bodily Activity	7 6 5 4 3 2 1	

ASSIGNMENT B-10

Aim of assignment: To experiment with the projection of an opinion of your own to the audience.

Type of performance: Select for a speech a subject upon which you have a deep conviction, belief, or opinion, the type of subject which makes you angry when it is mentioned. Present your opinion with all the depth of feeling which you have upon the subject. Make this feeling apparent to the audience. Transfer it to them.

Length of performance: Not more than three minutes.

Reference material: Review "Choice of Thought" and "Organization of Material" in this handbook.

Specific method: State the opinion you wish to present in the form of the central thought of your speech. Prepare your speech as suggested in previous assignments, following the seven-step pattern. Practice its presentation in order that you may project your feelings clearly and effectively. Be more interested in making your audience aware of your opinion and your feelings toward it than of the reasons for your belief.

Repeated functions: The speech should meet the test of a well-organized speech as outlined previously. Be sure that the central thought is well stated. Exaggerate the interpretation of your feelings. Follow your audience reaction. Control your projection in terms of their reaction.

Suggestions: Use the first person when you speak. Fill your speech with personal phrases such as "I think" or "I believe." Concentrate on your central thought. Be sure that you make your point of view clear and emphatic. Avoid generalization that is not directly related to your central thought.

B-10 EVALUATION

Date _____   Student _____

Subject _____

		COMMENTS:
Choice of Subject	7 6 5 4 3 2 1	
Choice of Thought	7 6 5 4 3 2 1	
Choice of Material	7 6 5 4 3 2 1	
Organization of Material	7 6 5 4 3 2 1	
Use of Language	7 6 5 4 3 2 1	
Projection to the Audience	7 6 5 4 3 2 1	
Control of Bodily Activity	7 6 5 4 3 2 1	
Rhythm	7 6 5 4 3 2 1	
Pronunciation	7 6 5 4 3 2 1	
Voice Control	7 6 5 4 3 2 1	

33   Assignments in the Essential Skills of Reading Aloud

The assignments below are designed to help you develop your skill in the essentials of reading aloud.

Again, as with the assignments on speech making, your instructor may wish to vary the procedure with your class by making a pertinent selection of the exercises suitable to your needs and abilities. Or he may wish to repeat any of significant value.

To be assured of a measure of success, check your selection of poems to read with your instructor. He will help you know whether your poem will help meet the aim of the assignment.

ASSIGNMENT C-1

Aim of assignment: To aid you in projection of thought in reading aloud.

Type of performance: Select a poem or poems you like, that your audience will like to hear you read aloud. Select a poem that has significant thought content. Avoid narrative poetry, the type that tells a story. It would be best to have a serious poem. *Read from the printed page.*

Length of performance: Not more than two minutes.

Reference material: Read "Projection of Thought," Section 25.

Specific method: Study your poem intently. Know the meaning of each phrase and word. Be able to express the central thought in your own

C-1 EVALUATION

Date _____   Student _____

Selection _____   Author _____

Choice of Material	7 6 5 4 3 2 1	COMMENTS:
Arrangement		
(Introduction)	7 6 5 4 3 2 1	
Projection of Thought	7 6 5 4 3 2 1	
Control of Bodily Activity	7 6 5 4 3 2 1	
Rhythm	7 6 5 4 3 2 1	
Pronunciation	7 6 5 4 3 2 1	
Voice Control	7 6 5 4 3 2 1	

words. Be sure you can read it in phrases, regardless of line scheme or rhyme scheme. It would be good for your reading if you were to type out your manuscript. If you do, it is not necessary to adhere to the line arrangement of the original. You are aiming to project thought. Decide on places where you should pause. Mark those places. Select key words to receive emphasis. Underline these words.

Suggestions: Prepare an introduction in which you mention the title, the author, and the central thought of the poem. Practice reading from manuscript.

ASSIGNMENT C-2

Aim of assignment: To approach the problem of *projection of emotion.*

Type of performance: Select a poem you like, one that your audience will like to hear you read aloud. Choose a simple narrative type of poem with thought and emotion expressed in broad sweeps through the use of many vivid and colorful words. It may be either serious or humorous. *Read from the printed page.*

Length of performance: Not more than two minutes.

Reference material: Study "Projection of Emotion," Section 26.

Specific method: Study the poem to ascertain its thought and emotional content. Estimate the reaction that the listener should give to the poem, its words, phrases, and stanzas. Plan your interpretation to secure that reaction. Try as hard as you can to define each word through the use of your voice by varying pitch, intensity, quality, and duration to suit your purpose. Make each word ring with its fullest meaning.

Repeated functions: Make sure of the meaning of all words and phrases. Mark your manuscript for pauses and emphasis.

Suggestions: Study the reactions of your audience. Estimate their interest and how closely they follow you. If they are restless or bored, you are not projecting adequately. You must sense a feeling of interest on

C-2 EVALUATION

Date _____   Student _____

Selection _____   Author _____

Arrangement							
(Introduction)	7 6 5 4 3 2 1		COMMENTS:				
Projection of Thought	7 6 5 4 3 2 1						
Projection of Emotion	7 6 5 4 3 2 1						
Bodily Activity	7 6 5 4 3 2 1						
Rhythm	7 6 5 4 3 2 1						
Pronunciation	7 6 5 4 3 2 1						
Voice Control	7 6 5 4 3 2 1						

their part. They must respond to you and the ideas of the poem with real interest and enthusiasm. Avoid merely reading aloud, in which you simply pronounce the words. Read *to* and *for* the audience.

ASSIGNMENT C-3

Aim of assignment: To experiment further with the development of effectiveness in *projection of thought* and *emotion.*

Type of performance: Choose a different type of poem for this performance. If you used a serious poem before, use a humorous poem this time. *Read from the printed page.*

Length of performance: Not more than two minutes.

Reference material: Review "Projection of Thought" and "Projection of Emotions."

Specific method: Repeat the method used in Assignments C-1 and C-2. Introduce your poem with a few brief remarks stating the name of the poem, its author, its source, and your reason for reading it. Try to stimulate your audience so that they respond with a great deal of interest and enthusiasm.

Repeated functions: Make each word and phrase vivid with thought and feeling. Make the audience aware of your endeavor to interpret the meaning attached to each word.

Suggestions: Practice the poem aloud many times. Become so familiar with it that you need only refer to the book for the exact wording of the poem. Experiment with different effects as you practice. In the production of your effects try the use of different pitch, quality, intensity, and duration changes. *Experiment as you practice.* Experiment with your audience as you read. Watch your audience for their response. If they do not respond, project more intently.

C-3 EVALUATION

Date _____   Student _____

Selection _____   Author _____

Choice of Material	7 6 5 4 3 2 1	COMMENTS:
Arrangement of Material	7 6 5 4 3 2 1	
Projection of Thought	7 6 5 4 3 2 1	
Projection of Emotion	7 6 5 4 3 2 1	
Bodily Activity	7 6 5 4 3 2 1	
Rhythm	7 6 5 4 3 2 1	
Pronunciation	7 6 5 4 3 2 1	
Voice Control	7 6 5 4 3 2 1	

Aim of assignment: To give further experience in the development of a style of projection to the audience, by combining speaking and reading in one performance.

Type of performance: Select a poem, several quotations from a long poem, or poems that express a thought you wish to present to the audience. Prepare a speech with this thought as the central thought and use the poetry as your material in developing the thought. Thus, you read and speak in the same performance.

Length of performance: Not more than three minutes.

Reference material: Review "Organization of Material" and "Projection of Thought" as outlined in this handbook.

Specific method: Follow in preparation of this speech the method you have previously learned. Practice reading the poetry aloud until you are confident of your ability to project its inner, deeper, richer meanings. Practice the entire performance until you make your speaking as vivid and colorful as your reading. Interpret every word and phrase with its proper emotional value. Let your own feelings be expressed completely whether you use your own words or the words of another.

Repeated functions: Your speech should have four parts and be built together as a unit. You should consider the reaction you wish to gain from your audience and strive to accomplish it. Exaggerate your interpretation sufficiently to make it clear.

Suggestions: Make use of proper transitions, in which you relate to your main thought the points involved in the poetry you read. Actually use the poetry in developing your thought. Try to project as well when you speak as when you read. Don't let a noticeable difference be apparent.

C-4 EVALUATION

Date _____   Student _____

Subject _____

Selection of Subject	7	6	5	4	3	2	1	COMMENTS:
Selection of Poetry	7	6	5	4	3	2	1	
Central Thought	7	6	5	4	3	2	1	
Organization (Introduction, Transitions, Conclusion)	7	6	5	4	3	2	1	
Projection of Thought and	7	6	5	4	3	2	1	
Emotion in the Poetry	7	6	5	4	3	2	1	
Rhythm, Pronunciation, and Voice Control	7	6	5	4	3	2	1	
Bodily Activity	7	6	5	4	3	2	1	

VII PROJECTS IN SPEAKING AND READING

34 Assignments Related to the
Cultural Context of Speech

This series of assignments is designed to emphasize the relationship between a speaker and his times. Public speaking is placed in a cultural context. Important events of the day bring important speeches from important people. We start with a historical review of a particular year. Next we note the great problems of the year, the speakers who talked about them, and where the speeches were delivered. Third, we examine one of those major speeches in terms of the occasion on which it was presented, who was in the audience, and the main points the speaker made.

Then we come to the present time. Our class members will go individually to hear a speaker. We may not hear a nationally famous individual, but we shall choose one who uses a current topic and who has a background that qualifies him to speak on it. We shall observe his audience and their reaction to him.

ASSIGNMENT D-1   "This Was the Year That Was."

Let everyone in the class select a different year and find out what happened in the world that year. Try encyclopedia yearbooks, newspaper files, and college newspaper files. Write a speech-essay of 500–700 words on the year. Include international, national, state, local, hometown, and campus activities. Include yourself and your family in it, if possible. Organize it well. Review Sections 14 and 16 on "Central Thought" and "Organization of Material."

Prepare a manuscript for reading aloud: one side of the page; typed, lettered, or readable script; double- or triple-spaced; no carry-over sentences from page to page. Rehearse the reading to be heard and understood. Work your sources into the text. Review Section 16 on "Manuscripts."

On the appointed day, give a note to the chairman, showing your name and year. Give this handbook to him. When called, take your seat at the front of the room. When introduced, step to the reading stand, arrange your manuscript for reading, and read the paper. After the meeting, turn in the manuscript. An evaluator will score your presentation on the following blank.

D-1 EVALUATION

Date _____   Student _____

Year _____

Followed Assignment Instructions	7 6 5 4 3 2 1	COMMENTS:
Content (Interesting, Varied, Personal)	7 6 5 4 3 2 1	
Quality of Writing (Clear, Coherent, "Oral")	7 6 5 4 3 2 1	
Use of Voice (Audible, Understandable)	7 6 5 4 3 2 1	
Bodily Action (Handled Script Well)	7 6 5 4 3 2 1	
Skill in Reading	7 6 5 4 3 2 1	
Quality of Manuscript	7 6 5 4 3 2 1	

ASSIGNMENT D-2   "Speakers and Speeches in _____"

Using *Vital Speeches* as your principal source, discover the major topics that were used for speeches during your year. (*Vital Speeches* is the name of a periodical containing the texts of speeches. You will find it in your school library. Most of the publications will be in bound volumes, grouped by years.) Who were the people who made speeches on these topics? Where were the speeches given? List them here:

Topics (the problems of the day)

Occasions (what groups heard the major speeches)

Speakers (who made the significant speeches)

Main points (give the central thought of each speech you list)

Prepare to speak for three minutes on these four items. For notes to use while speaking, prepare four 4-by-6 cards, each devoted to one of the above four categories. On the day assigned, notify the chairman of your name and year. When introduced, come to the speaker's stand. Stand beside it. Keep your cards in your hands and use them during the talk. Turn in the note cards after the speech. As you begin speaking, point out the connection between this talk and your speech in Assignment D-1. This becomes your introduction. You will not have this material on cards. Have it well planned.

D-2 EVALUATION

Date _____   Student _____

"Speakers and Speeches in _____"

Followed Assignment		COMMENTS:
Instructions	7 6 5 4 3 2 1	
Tie-in with First Speech	7 6 5 4 3 2 1	
Transitions and Conclusion	7 6 5 4 3 2 1	
Visible Presentation (Posture, Handling Note Cards)	7 6 5 4 3 2 1	
Quality of Note Cards	7 6 5 4 3 2 1	

ASSIGNMENT D-3   "A Speaker of Note"

Select one speech from your year, as reported in your speech in Assignment D-2. Prepare to talk to the class for four minutes, including the points listed below. Then add another point: What evidence do you have that the speech was successful? Did the audience applaud? Is the speech interesting to read? Give samples of the language used by reading a passage at least fifty words long. Can you evaluate the speaker's use of language from this sample? Was it ear-catching, clear, direct, complex, confusing, dull? Try to spend at least half of your time on the audience, the occasion, and who the speaker was. As you think of him, tell us why you think he was invited to speak to this audience. Do you think he was qualified to speak on his subject?

Year _____ Speaker _____ Topic _____

Audience _____ Occasion _____ Source _____

For this speech, prepare two pages of speaker's notes: full-sized sheets, typed or legibly written on one side only. Place introductory remarks at the top. Write out each main point in complete sentences. Let all supporting material be written in phrases of not more than five or six words. Underline key words.

On the day assigned, tell the chairman your name and the name of the speaker you will talk about. When introduced, place your two pages of notes side by side on the lectern. Leave them there during the talk. Try to move around to the side for part of your speech. At the conclusion of the hour, turn in the notes.

D-3 EVALUATION

Date _____   Student _____

Title: _____   Made an Important Speech in _____

Followed Assignment	7	6	5	4	3	2	1	*COMMENTS:*
Content (Was the "speak-ing situation" kept foremost?)	7	6	5	4	3	2	1	
Use of Notes	7	6	5	4	3	2	1	
Suitable Speech Sample	7	6	5	4	3	2	1	
Treatment of "Successful Speech" Idea	7	6	5	4	3	2	1	
Visible Presentation (Movement)	7	6	5	4	3	2	1	
Quality of Notes	7	6	5	4	3	2	1	

ASSIGNMENT D-4   "A Local Speaker"

Attend a speech on campus, at a service club, at a convention, or on another occasion. Avoid a sermon, since it is difficult to evaluate a sermon with the same categories we use for other occasional speeches.

Prepare the same kind of speech for this assignment that you did for Assignment D-3, except for the personal references you will include. Indicate how the speaker looked and sounded. Describe the audience: its size, attitude, composition, response, and so forth. What were the main points of the speech? How about the speaker's use of language? How did the audience respond to the talk? Was the speaker qualified to speak on his subject?

Prepare the same kind of notes as you did for Assignment D-3. Turn them in at the end of the hour.

D-4 EVALUATION

Date _____   Student _____

Title: "I Went to Hear _____"

		COMMENTS:
Treatment of Local Situation	7 6 5 4 3 2 1	
Content of Speech (Including Personal References)	7 6 5 4 3 2 1	
Evaluation of Speech	7 6 5 4 3 2 1	
Use of Notes	7 6 5 4 3 2 1	
Oral Presentation	7 6 5 4 3 2 1	
Visible Presentation	7 6 5 4 3 2 1	
Quality of Notes	7 6 5 4 3 2 1	

35   *Speaking Assignments Related to a Field or Profession*

This series of speech assignments is designed for a class in business and professional speaking. These speeches should help prepare you meet those occasions when, as a professional person, you may be asked to make a talk to a service club or a high school career day about your field of work; to speak at an annual banquet for company employees; to address a conference or meeting within your professional association or a dinner honoring a member of your profession; to conduct a job interview; to participate in a group discussion; or to speak to a local civic club about a problem that needs a solution.

ASSIGNMENT E-1   Exposition on a Field of Work

Consider your business or profession—the one you are training for. Prepare a five-minute speech of three to five main points. In one point, identify your field in the world of business or the professions in the United

States. Next, indicate the type of training people can get for the work. Then indicate the nature of your participation in it. How you have become interested, whether you have worked in it or are now doing so, and what the opportunities are. Prepare an outline as you work on this speech. Follow the pattern in Section 16 in this handbook. Try to have at least one visual aid to display during your talk. Review Section 15 on visual aids.

On the day assigned, give this rating blank and your outline to the evaluator. Discuss the use of your visual aid with the chairman: whether you need the blackboard or an easel; if so, where you want it; and where you will keep your materials until you are ready to show them. When introduced, come to the speaker's stand. At the opportune time show your visual aid. At the conclusion of the speech be sure the visual aid is removed.

E-1 EVALUATION

Date _____   Student _____

Choice of Subject and Personal Association	7 6 5 4 3 2 1	*COMMENTS:*
Content Suited to Audience	7 6 5 4 3 2 1	
Organization (Introduction, Transitions, Conclusion)	7 6 5 4 3 2 1	
Use of Language	7 6 5 4 3 2 1	
Quality and Use of Visual Aid	7 6 5 4 3 2 1	
Oral Presentation	7 6 5 4 3 2 1	
Visual Presentation	7 6 5 4 3 2 1	
Quality of Outline	7 6 5 4 3 2 1	

ASSIGNMENT E-2   Some Historical Notes

Who knows of an organization that does not have a Founder's Day, or an Annual Banquet, or an Awards Ceremony, or a Farewell Dinner? Imagine such an occasion for an organization in your field.

Prepare a six-minute speech which traces the history of some firm, organization, movement, or activity during a period of its existence. Plan the organization very carefully. Essentially it will be a time-sequence speech. Group the events into three or four groups. Place yourself in the speech somewhere and acknowledge the source of your information. A visual aid might serve well.

Write out the complete manuscript for oral presentation. Companies like to have this type of manuscript for publication in company magazines. Review the section on speech manuscripts in this handbook as you prepare. Then place the manuscript in some type of binder, so that it can remain bound together but have the pages loose to be turned as the speech proceeds. Turn in the manuscript and binder after the meeting. They will be returned to you.

Read the speech from the manuscript in the binder, remembering to maintain good eye contact.

E-2 EVALUATION

Date _____   Student _____

Title: _____

		COMMENTS:
Choice of Subject	7 6 5 4 3 2 1	COMMENTS:
Content (Identifying Sources and Relating Personal Association)	7 6 5 4 3 2 1	
Organization	7 6 5 4 3 2 1	
Use of Language	7 6 5 4 3 2 1	
Oral Presentation	7 6 5 4 3 2 1	
Visible Presentation (Including Handling of Manuscript)	7 6 5 4 3 2 1	
Quality of Manuscript	7 6 5 4 3 2 1	

ASSIGNMENT E-3   The Progress Report

In nearly every business or profession people make reports on the progress that is being made with certain projects. Prepare a six-minute speech which traces the steps in the progress of some project in your field, for example, the development of the physical facilities for the home economics department or the development of the plans for a park, or a swimming pool, or a Lion's Club barbecue.

Prepare a handout to be distributed to the class. On this handout you will have only a series of dates with identifying titles, such as the following:

Progress Report on Our Debate Tournament

4-21-69	Decision to hold debate tournament
6-10-69	Formulating plans
7-2-69	Letters of inquiry sent
2-4-70	Local arrangements completed
3-26-70	Invitations mailed
7-27-70	Committees formed
9-4-70	Entry blanks mailed
10-14-70	Everything is ready

Review the section on visual aids in this handbook. Do not prepare any type of speaker's notes to take with you to the speaker's stand. Use a copy of your handout, with some added notes, if you like, to remind you of things you want to say.

On the day assigned, come to the front of the room and when called upon, come to the speaker's stand. Present your introduction from the side of the stand. Then, when you reach the point of stating the central idea for the speech, bring out your handouts from a briefcase or the speaker's box or from off the table. Ask someone to assist you in passing them out.

People will now be looking at the handouts. Continue talking. For example, call their attention to how certain items can be grouped together. The above example could have about four groups of two dates. Then proceed with the talk, point by point. Turn in your copy of the handout after the speech.

E-3 EVALUATION

Date _____   Student _____

Title _____

		COMMENTS:
Appropriateness of Subject and Content	7 6 5 4 3 2 1	
Organization and Grouping	7 6 5 4 3 2 1	
Use of Language	7 6 5 4 3 2 1	
Oral Presentation	7 6 5 4 3 2 1	
Visible Presentation	7 6 5 4 3 2 1	
Quality of Handout	7 6 5 4 3 2 1	

ASSIGNMENT E-4   The Speech of Tribute

There are many occasions on which a person is recognized for the outstanding contributions he has made to his field. Sometimes the speeches are made in his presence when an award is to be given. That speech is often short and might be called a speech of presentation. For this assign-

E-4 EVALUATION

Date _____   Student _____

Title: A tribute to _____

		COMMENTS:
Choice of Person and Central Thought	7 6 5 4 3 2 1	
Organization (Transitions)	7 6 5 4 3 2 1	
Supporting Materials	7 6 5 4 3 2 1	
Use of Language	7 6 5 4 3 2 1	
Pronunciation and Articulation	7 6 5 4 3 2 1	
Bodily Activity and Handling Manuscript	7 6 5 4 3 2 1	
Quality of Manuscript	7 6 5 4 3 2 1	

ment we think more specifically of the occasion when the person is not present. If the person is no longer living, the speech is called a "eulogy." Study Section 37 in this handbook for suggestions on content and organization.

Select a person you have known personally. If this is impossible, then select someone in your field who is widely known or someone about whom you can get first-hand information from someone else.

Prepare a typed manuscript. This could well be your finest effort in the use of language. Let the manuscript be about three pages long. When you read, do not hurry it. Be precise, careful, and deliberate in articulation and pronunciation. After the speech turn in the manuscript.

ASSIGNMENT E-5   The Job Interview

People who want jobs apply for them. Let us watch some of our classmates in a role-playing job interview.

Select a partner—someone from the same profession you are in. Let the "applicant" of the pair decide on the type of job for which he is applying. Let the "employer" prepare an application blank for the position and let the applicant fill it out. It will be on the employer's desk during the interview. Hand it in after the classroom presentation.

On presentation day, let the pair arrange the stage with the understanding of the chairman. Then the applicant tells the class what the situation is and he leaves the room. When the employer is ready, someone designated as the secretary will bring in the applicant and the interview is on. Plan to terminate in no more than ten minutes. The applicant will leave.

E-5 EVALUATION

Type of job _____   Date _____

Applicant _____   Employer _____

Applicant		Employer
Appropriateness of Attitude	7 6 5 4 3 2 1	Appropriateness of Attitude
Quality of Questions Asked	7 6 5 4 3 2 1	Quality of Replies
Quality of Replies	7 6 5 4 3 2 1	Quality of Questions Asked
Evidence of Preparation	7 6 5 4 3 2 1	Evidence of Preparation
Bodily Action	7 6 5 4 3 2 1	Bodily Action
Use of Voice	7 6 5 4 3 2 1	Use of Voice
For Filling Out Application	7 6 5 4 3 2 1	Quality of Application Form

ASSIGNMENT E-6   Group Discussion

People in business and the professions gather for meetings where they hear "groups" discuss problems, plans, new ideas, procedures, and so forth. Check several times with the instructor as you help organize a group of people in your business or profession.

Let the group select a topic and phrase a discussion question. (Examples: Should cigarette advertising be removed from newspapers? Does industry have an interest in the free-time activity of its employees? How should the legal profession look at "no fault" car insurance?)

Select a chairman. Develop an outline for the discussion. Suggested divisions for the outline might be: (1) Introductions, (2) The conditions as they are, (3) Goals to achieve, (4) Possible solutions, (5) Which seems to be the best plan? (6) Is there something we can do about it?

Plan for six minutes times the number of participants (for example, twenty-four minutes for four people). Arrange the front of the room so that you sit behind tables facing the audience. Try to contribute at each point of the outline. After the presentation, turn in the outline. Participants can be evaluated on the blank below. The chairman needs additional evaluative criteria, such as: (1) tried to get everyone to participate; (2) good summaries; (3) kept within the time scheme.

E-6 EVALUATION

Date _____   Student _____

Discussion problem: _____

Contributions (Questions, Answers, Ideas, Statements)	7 6 5 4 3 2 1	COMMENTS:
Keeping on the Track (Avoided Interruptions, Regressions, Jumping Ahead)	7 6 5 4 3 2 1	
Cooperativeness with Others	7 6 5 4 3 2 1	
Use of Voice	7 6 5 4 3 2 1	
Clarity of Proposal or Suggestions	7 6 5 4 3 2 1	
Ability to Analyze	7 6 5 4 3 2 1	
Quality of Outline (Group Work)	7 6 5 4 3 2 1	

ASSIGNMENT E-7   Persuasion (Problem-Solution Speech)

The professions and the business world have problems. Sometimes they can be settled internally, but other times they are handled by society, for example, labor disputes, socialized medicine, no-fault auto insurance, inflation, cigarette advertising, farm subsidies, social welfare, and federal aid to education.

Select some problem which affects your field. Consider it well and decide on the solution you would propose. Let that be the central thought of your speech. For suggestions, study Assignment G-2 in Section 37.

Prepare speaker's notes for this speech (no complete manuscripts or outlines). Use either cards or full sheets of paper.

On your day to speak, notify the chairman of your title and take your seat. When you are introduced, come to the speaker's stand, lay down your notes, look at the audience, recognize the chairman by name, and begin. This is a persuasive speech. Do your very best to use the available means of persuasion.

E-7 EVALUATION

Date _____   Student _____

Title _____

		COMMENTS:
Choice of Subject	7 6 5 4 3 2 1	
Choice of Thought	7 6 5 4 3 2 1	
Choice of Material	7 6 5 4 3 2 1	
Organization of Material	7 6 5 4 3 2 1	
Use of Language	7 6 5 4 3 2 1	
Control of Bodily Activity	7 6 5 4 3 2 1	
Rhythm and Pronunciation	7 6 5 4 3 2 1	
Use of Voice	7 6 5 4 3 2 1	

ASSIGNMENT E-8   The Research Report

Many business people report on material which has been printed. We now have an opportunity to practice this type of activity.

Select an article from a professional journal in your field. Get advice for the selection from your instructor. **Note:** In some classes, students

E-8 EVALUATION

Date _____   Student _____

Topic _____   Source of article _____

		COMMENTS:
Introduction (Reference to Subject in Field)	7 6 5 4 3 2 1	
Handout (Clarity, Completeness)	7 6 5 4 3 2 1	
Content (Related to Audience)	7 6 5 4 3 2 1	
Organization (Main Points Clear)	7 6 5 4 3 2 1	
Visual Presentation (Communicativeness)	7 6 5 4 3 2 1	
Oral Presentation ("Speech-like" Quality)	7 6 5 4 3 2 1	
Conclusion (Summary, Tie-in)	7 6 5 4 3 2 1	
Quality of Handout	7 6 5 4 3 2 1	

may wish to read collaterally, on material related to Part II of this handbook. Use such material for this speech, if your instructor approves.

Prepare a ten-minute report on the material. Let it be a speech with a well-prepared introduction, body, and conclusion.

Prepare a handout in the form of a skeletal outline of the material to be covered. Use not more than twenty lines on one page. Refer to the outline as you make your speech. Be sure to include in your introduction some remarks about the place of the material in your field or of the material in this course.

36 Incidentally Speaking

In this section there are three assignments, two of personal interest to you, and the third the impromptu speech. The first two could be used by you on some informal occasion, as a short, interesting, addition to a program. The impromptu speech is one anybody might have the impulse to give.

ASSIGNMENT F-1   "This Is My Day"

A person in business or a profession should have a pleasant little speech in his files—one that can be pulled out and used as a light, after-dinner speech. Here is something you might wish to develop.

F-1 EVALUATION

Date _____   Student _____

Title: My day is _____

		COMMENTS:
Interesting Content and Grouping	7 6 5 4 3 2 1	COMMENTS:
Opening Remarks, Transitions, and Conclusion	7 6 5 4 3 2 1	
Use of Voice	7 6 5 4 3 2 1	
Communicativeness (Facial Animation, Bodily Activity)	7 6 5 4 3 2 1	
Quality of Note Card	7 6 5 4 3 2 1	

Prepare a three-minute speech based on what has happened in the world on your birthday. Several plans may be considered: (1) Down through history, what has happened on that day? (2) What took place around the world on the very day you were born? (3) What other great people have the same birth date and what have they done? (4) What events in sports, or politics, or social reform, or whatever have taken place on your day and what was the significance to the world? Group your entries in three or four categories.

Help each other in the search for materials. Prepare a single note card, written on only one side.

When you are introduced, come to the front of the table or speaker's stand. Present your talk from there. Determine what you will do with the card and your hands and arms as you speak.

ASSIGNMENT F-2   "A Very Special Day"

Is there some day that has special meaning for you? How about Thanksgiving, St. Swithun's Day, Veteran's Day, Election Day, the day of the Rose Bowl, Arbor Day?

Prepare a short talk of not more than four minutes, making special reference to the significance of a particular day or of some aspect of that day's recognition, such as the history of Santa Claus at Christmas.

Select your topic, do your research, and prepare an outline for this speech. Use the "narrative" form of introduction. Hand in the outline before you speak.

Do not take your outline to the speaker's stand. Use note cards only. When you are introduced, recognize the chairman by name. If you can do so during the speech, refer to some member of the audience by name with an appropriate comment. Turn in your note cards after the meeting.

F-2 EVALUATION

Date _____   Student _____

Topic _____

"Narrative Introduction"	7	6	5	4	3	2	1	COMMENTS:
Subject and Personal Identification	7	6	5	4	3	2	1	
Central Idea and Relevant Organization	7	6	5	4	3	2	1	
Supporting Material	7	6	5	4	3	2	1	
Extemporaneous Presentation	7	6	5	4	3	2	1	
Audience Adaptation	7	6	5	4	3	2	1	
Quality of Outline and Cards	7	6	5	4	3	2	1	

ASSIGNMENT F-3   The Impromptu Speech

Almost everyone is called upon at some time to face an audience without having had an opportunity for extensive preparation. In fact, the more widely known a speaker becomes the more often he will be asked to "say a few words." We want to give you a chance to have this kind of speaking experience.

Expect to give a two-minute speech. There is no advance preparation that you need to make—or can make, for that matter—except to understand some of the things you can do to have a satisfying experience. Before you speak, for example, listen to what others are saying and open with a remark referring to what someone else has said. When you know what your topic is, don't waste time worrying that you can't say anything about it. Start thinking with some organizational pattern, such as: (1) think this about it. (2) Here is an example. (3) That's what I think. Or here's another, the one-point speech plan: (1) State a point, ask a question, disagree with a point, or agree with a point. (2) Support your statement.

Keep in mind that a speech has an ending. Try for a final statement—a summary, restatement of point, or plea for belief or action.

And, as has been said, "Stand up, speak up, shut up!"

Your instructor will work out with you the procedure to follow. He may use cards with topics on them. You draw two or three, select one, and walk to the front of the room, planning your speech on the way. Sometimes someone starts to talk about a particular topic and stops from time to time to say, "And what do you think about it, Mr. Jones?"

Be sure to give this handbook to your instructor at the beginning of the hour, so that he will have it ready to evaluate your speech when you are called on.

F-3 EVALUATION

Date _____   Student _____

Topic _____

		COMMENTS:
Central Idea and Supporting Material	7 6 5 4 3 2 1	
Opening and Closing	7 6 5 4 3 2 1	
Use of Language	7 6 5 4 3 2 1	
Rhythm and Pronunciation	7 6 5 4 3 2 1	
Voice and Bodily Activity	7 6 5 4 3 2 1	

37 The Long Speech

Among the objectives for a beginning course in speech are improving the basic processes of speech and increasing the student's ability in the basic skills of speech making and reading aloud. To do this we usually make assignments calling for very short performances. This makes for *speaking readiness.* It enables the student to meet speaking situations with enough understanding and "know-how" to have a go at his task with some degree of confidence.

In addition to the short assignments we make, we often wish that some of our students, who are ready for more advanced work, might have an opportunity to go on in developing the art of speaking. Therefore, we present now a series of assignments that will give these advanced students, who have already acquired some assurance and poise in their speaking, an opportunity to do longer, more careful, and more intense planning, preparation, and rehearsal than before.

In addition, the advanced student will consider his audience more closely. He need not be as much concerned about his own participation as a beginner. He can concentrate on eliciting desired responses from his listeners.

We do not intend through these assignments to give specific training in making speeches to meet particular occasions, such as the speech of welcome, the speech of presentation, the speech of acceptance, the after-dinner speech, reading the minutes of meetings of the club, or reading the scripture lesson for your young people's religious group. Neither do we plan to train anyone to do an oration for intercollegiate participation.

We do plan to encourage through the basic assignments a readiness to speak. And through these advanced assignments we hope you will learn that you too can give a good talk if you are willing to make the effort.

ASSIGNMENT G-1   The Speech to Inform

Aim of assignment: To provide the listener with information on a specific subject through presenting in detail, rehearsing industriously, and speaking extemporaneously an informative talk in a natural, spontaneous form. The listeners must be able to comprehend easily, be very much interested, and be able to remember what you said.

Length of performance: Between seven and ten minutes.

Method and suggestions: Consider carefully the skills of speech making, as follows:

Choice of subject—Remember that your audience will be your classmates and the occasion will be your class meeting, unless you and your instructor make arrangements for presenting the speech at a different time and place. Some groups like to meet in the evening, in some place other than the classroom, in groups of about eight students, devoting about an hour and a half to the meeting.

The topic you choose may require that you do any or all of the following: explain a process, a thing, or an idea; develop a principle or a theory; paint a word picture using words of vivid imagery; relate the events or series of events of a significant happening; or report the results of a survey or investigation. The speech should contain information that you are reasonably sure your audience does not already have. You should know a lot about it to begin with, know where you can find more, and be very much interested in it yourself.

Choice of thought—You need a central thought for this speech, as for any other. It should be clear and brief. It should be divided into points— probably not less than three nor more than five.

Choice of material—Decide on the type of supporting material you will use. If you decide to use statistics, get them. If you plan to use statements from authority, find them. Select your materials with your audience in mind. Make a sincere effort to use some of your information in the form of visual aids. This means charts, diagrams, mounted drawings and pictures. Be sure they are large enough to be seen from the back of the room.

Organization of material—Think out carefully the order of arrangement you plan to use—time, space, topical, or otherwise. Think out your transitional devices very carefully. Decide on the type of conclusion you wish to have, and plan it. Do the same for the introduction. Write out the first thirty-five words you will say after you have been introduced by the chairman. Do the same for the last words you will utter before you sit down.

Use of language—This speech is to be extemporaneous, to be sure. Yet there are places in any speech where you want to say exactly what you mean in the best language you can plan. Such places are at the opening, as you state the central thought and the subpoints, as you make your transitions, and as you finish. Be sure you know whether you must use any unusual or technical terms. If you must, be sure to include clear explanations of each or simplifications for them.

Projection to the audience—Plan for this speech. Consider where you will stand, the position you feel would be best for you. Then practice these things. Ask someone who is interested in the progress you are making to hear you practice your talk. Practice by yourself several times and then speak before this person, who will give you his appraisal of the talk. Your instructor would be your best critic, but a classmate or a member of your family could help. If it is a member of your family, you will want to "brief" him on what you are trying to do.

Be sure to "speak up" in the practice session and to look at your listener. Use as much voice as you think you will need when you are speaking to the audience for whom you have planned this talk. You cannot do this until you are ready, so be sure to practice several times first by yourself.

Control of bodily activity—Your activity in moving about and gesturing should arise out of your thought and feeling as you speak. By having visual aids you will enhance your control of bodily activity. Have the aids hung or placed before you begin to speak. Do not mention them until you are ready to use them. Uncover them as you need them. Recover them or remove them when you are through with them—usually during the speech, as you finish with them. Practice pointing out the features of the visual aids. Use the hand nearest the device as you stand to one side or the other.

Rhythm—It is often a good idea to intentionally increase the rate of your speaking in order to present an enthusiastic appearance to the audience and insure their attention. At the same time do not forget that pauses and variety in emphasis and inflection are among your most effective avenues to interestingness.

Pronunciation—Have your audience in mind. Do not allow yourself to use words you are unsure of. Many of your classmates will not respond favorably if you mispronounce words.

Voice control—Here again, think of your audience. They like to hear without effort. Be sure to speak a little louder than you sometimes do—unless you have been told that your voice is naturally too loud. In that rare event, make a sincere effort to cut down on volume. As you practice, try repeating some phrases several times in order to make sure that you are presenting the meaning you want to present in the best manner you are capable.

G-1 EVALUATION

Date _____   Student _____

Title _____

Choice of Subject	7	6	5	4	3	2	1	COMMENTS:
Choice of Thought	7	6	5	4	3	2	1	
Choice of Material	7	6	5	4	3	2	1	
Organization of Material	7	6	5	4	3	2	1	
Use of Language	7	6	5	4	3	2	1	
Projection to the Audience	7	6	5	4	3	2	1	
Control of Bodily Activity	7	6	5	4	3	2	1	
Rhythm	7	6	5	4	3	2	1	
Pronunciation	7	6	5	4	3	2	1	
Voice Control	7	6	5	4	3	2	1	

ASSIGNMENT G-2   A Speech to Persuade

Aim of assignment: To provide practice under close supervision in the gathering, evaluation, and use of evidence (such as examples, statistics, and testimony) to convince others of the soundness of a point of view which you hold.

Length of performance: From seven to ten minutes.

Method and suggestions: Probably you use persuasion throughout life more than you use exposition (giving information). Think of what you do during the day: you try to get your car pool to be on time in the morning, you try to get a friend to go over to the student center with you to get a cup of coffee before the next class, you try to get a student to lend you his notes for the class you missed, you try to get your father to lend you his car for the evening. All of these efforts to influence the action of others are a form of persuasion. Think of the times you argue a point, trying to get someone to agree with you. This is persuasion.

This assignment calls for your best efforts, again following the guiding considerations of the essential skills of speech making.

Choice of subject—Select your subject carefully. Before making your final selection, talk with your instructor to make sure you are on the right track. Pick a topic from among the many problems of international, national, state, local, or campus scope. Be sure there is controversy about it and that you have heard some arguments on both sides. When you are sure that you have a problem that has two sides, think about it with a sincere effort to decide which side you really believe in. Then make sure that information on your side is available. For this speech you will not be able to call entirely on your own experiences and information.

Choice of thought—You know which side of the argument you are on. Now state what you believe in definite, clear terms. This statement becomes your central thought. Make it specific. Let it clearly ask your audience to believe something. For example, do not state your central thought like this: "Abortion laws should be changed." Make it specific, more like this: "The United States government should establish a uniform nationwide abortion law."

Then set down all the "reasons" you can think of. These reasons become the main points of your speech. If you have more than five you probably will not have time to prove each one. It would be better to combine some or leave some out and do a good job of proving the important ones you have settled on.

Choice of material—You will need to collect evidence for each of your reasons. You will need to read on the subject, searching for facts, statistics, examples, illustrations, and quotations for each reason. You want your audience to agree with you. They won't, if all you can do is make assertions without backing them up with evidence. But if you have the facts and figures, they will be more likely to accept your proof.

Organization of material—You will need to arrange your main points in the best possible order. The same is true for the supporting material and the details of the supporting material.

When you have assembled all the evidence for one reason and have arranged it, plan a summary of it, showing what you have accomplished. This is a type of transition to the next main reason.

Plan your conclusion carefully, making sure that it repeats all your main reasons, which led you to the point of view that you have and that you expressed in your central thought. Finally, restate your point.

Plan your introduction to show the importance of the problem that you are going to discuss. Tell something of the background of the problem—how it started, how you became interested in it, how the audience is affected by it—and then state your central idea and point out the main reasons for your position.

Get your argument down on paper in the form of an outline—called a "brief" in argumentation. Show your brief to your instructor for approval before you begin rehearsing your speech.

Use of language—In this speech you must use exact, forceful, clear words. Omit vague words unless you define them for your listeners. Be sure that you have the central thought and main points carefully worded so that they say exactly what you want them to say. When you rehearse, insist that you present these points in the words you planned. Your audience is not likely to agree unless you use unmistakable language.

Projection to the audience—Sincerity is the key to your success here. If you are sincere you will be able to practice a well-prepared, well-documented speech. If you are sincere you will be able to rehearse a speech that expresses your own convictions. Keep this sincerity.

Be enthusiastic without bombast. Step up the rate of some of the delivery without ranting. Be loud without shouting.

Again, as in the speech to inform, ask someone to listen to a rehearsal. Talk *to* this critic, not *at* him. It is hard at first, but the practice will make it easier to talk to your audience later.

Control of bodily activity—Moving about the platform and gesturing are part of speaking. During your early rehearsals exaggerate your movement and gestures. Then as you go on rehearsing, be selective, just as you are selective in your use of words. Just because you are enthusiastic, do not let it run away with you to the point where you fling your arms wildly. Be sincerely enthusiastic.

Rhythm—Again you may speak a little faster than usual. Lots of persuaders do, especially when they are as well prepared as you want to be for this speech. But keep your speaking rhythm controlled. Be careful of just racing along. Remember the pause and variety.

Pronunciation—Make sure of the pronunciation of the words you use.

Voice control—Sometimes speakers tend to raise their pitch when they are earnestly arguing. Be careful that your voice does not reach a high pitch and stay there. Practice making your voice do what you want it to do. In the enthusiasm of your argument, do not forget that an effective voice will help dispose an audience favorably to you and to your argument.

G-2 EVALUATION

Date _____   Student _____

Title _____

Choice of Subject	7	6	5	4	3	2	1	COMMENTS:
Choice of Thought	7	6	5	4	3	2	1	
Choice of Material	7	6	5	4	3	2	1	
Organization of Material	7	6	5	4	3	2	1	
Use of Language	7	6	5	4	3	2	1	
Projection to the Audience	7	6	5	4	3	2	1	
Control of Bodily Activity	7	6	5	4	3	2	1	
Rhythm	7	6	5	4	3	2	1	
Pronunciation	7	6	5	4	3	2	1	
Voice Control	7	6	5	4	3	2	1	

ASSIGNMENT G-3   The Eulogy

Today, more and more people have the chance to read a speech they have written themselves. This is particularly true of people who appear on television. Many people speaking in public wish to be very careful to say exactly what they mean. For an assignment in this course, the eulogy may serve very well. It has before. Perhaps your instructor will substitute another type of speech to write out in full.

Aim of assignment: To provide practice in writing a speech, with emphasis on choice of language and speech composition; and to provide further opportunity to rehearse carefully for the purpose of reading aloud from the printed page.

Length of performance: Seven to ten minutes.

Method and suggestions: Follow the basic skills for speech composition and reading aloud. Your performance will be enjoyed by your audience mainly as an oral reading.

Choice of subject—The eulogy is a speech in praise of the accomplishments or personal characteristics of some person no longer living. For this assignment, we ask that you select someone you have known personally or someone among your own ancestors. This means that many of you will pick a grandfather or grandmother, an uncle or aunt, perhaps a parent or a brother or sister. By doing this you will have the most real speaking situation of the course. It goes far beyond the usual classroom assignment, because you are so closely concerned. In some families there are members of earlier generations who are still talked about with praise by the present members. You may wish to talk about that person. Or it may be that in your home town there was a person whom you knew, and about whom you would like to write and deliver a eulogy.

Choice of thought—You need a central thought. It is successfully stated as: "My grandfather lived by a simple rule of life" or "My aunt had traits of character that made her beloved by all who knew her" or "We remember our small cousin for her sweet disposition." You will think of the specific central idea that applies to the person you are eulogizing. Then you must decide on the subpoints. These will often be incidents from your subject's life that illustrate your central thought.

Choice of material and organization of material—Somewhere in the course of the speech, perhaps early, you will need to give certain facts about the life of your individual—his birth, education, occupation, achievements, and death. From then on you may spend your time presenting instances from his life that illustrate the central thought and main subpoints.

When your preparation has reached this point, get it down on paper in outline form. Show it to your instructor for his criticism.

Use of language—You now are ready to do some writing. This is where the difficulty comes. You will be tempted to write an essay. But if you were to try to present a talk from your outline notes—and if you should record that speech on a tape recorder, you would find that you do not speak like an essay. Spoken sentences are shorter than written sentences. Words are simpler. There are times when you speak fragmentary groups of words, incomplete sentences. Your oral composition has informalities about it—contractions and personal pronouns—that you don't use in an essay.

If you do not have a tape recorder on which you can tape your speech and from which you can later transcribe it, then try this: speak through the talk once, all the way. This will put it briefly in mind. Then say it aloud again. Go very slowly, trying as you do to write fast enough to get down what you said. Use any kind of shorthand or speedwriting that you can.

Now, write or type this first draft. Show it to your instructor for criticism of organization and choice of material and thought.

Next, work over the composition, smoothing out grammatical inaccuracies. Check for unnecessary repetitions. Work over your use of words. You want it to sound like you talking, but you should want it to sound like you at your sincere, cultured best. Write out this second draft. Submit it for evaluation of your use of words.

Let the third draft be prepared for the speaker's stand. Ask yourself some questions as you are doing this preparation: Have I said exactly what I want to say? Are my words, phrases, and sentences specific? Am I using varied language? Does it sound like me talking? Are my sentences too long or too short? Is there variety in the composition? And finally, check to see that you have given dignity and beauty to your use of language.

Projection to the audience—You will find that you are sincere. You are talking about someone near to you. You may wish to be more reserved and quiet for this speech than for some others you have made.

Projection of thought—The thoughts are your own. The writing is your own. Projection of thought will not give you difficulty.

Projection of emotion—There will be emotional content in this talk. The audience will realize the closeness of the person to you. You will not have difficulty. And if you have rehearsed the presentation enough times, you will not be surprised by the sound of your voice in an emotional passage. For some this is a disturbing experience. They are actually living the emotion at the moment. Be sure to rehearse it many times.

Control of bodily activity—Use a well-lighted reading stand for the speech. Practice with your manuscript. Have a typed paper, double- or triple-spaced. Learn to slide the pages to the side rather than turn them over.

Limit your bodily action. Stand still. You probably will not need gestures. Your face will reflect your thinking well enough. You need not practice facial expressions for this speech. Practice looking up as though at the audience as you read.

Rhythm—This will be controlled by your thought and feeling during the reading. The important thing is that the speech should sound like you when you talk. If you have read it aloud frequently when you were writing it, you probably have a fine rhythm established.

Pronunciation—Be correct, accurate, clear, and dignified.

G-3 EVALUATION

Date _____   Student _____

Subject _____

		COMMENTS:
Choice of Subject	7 6 5 4 3 2 1	
Use of Language	7 6 5 4 3 2 1	
Central Thought and Supporting Material	7 6 5 4 3 2 1	
Organization	7 6 5 4 3 2 1	
Skill in Reading	7 6 5 4 3 2 1	
Rhythm and Pronunciation	7 6 5 4 3 2 1	
Bodily Activity Handling Script	7 6 5 4 3 2 1	

Voice control—You probably will naturally keep the pitch of your voice low. Read easily and quietly. Use a narrow range of intensity. Just be sure that those in the rear are able to hear.

38   The Long Oral Reading

It is likely that most of your opportunities to read aloud will call for short readings, such as reading the minutes of a meeting or reading the Scriptures.

There may be an occasion, however, when you will be called upon to present a special feature at your club meeting. In that event the following assignments of the longer reading may help you face those occasions with greater confidence and poise. You might find a rather keen interest in reading aloud and want to take more course work in interpretation.

ASSIGNMENT G-4   Reading Prose Aloud

Aim of the assignment: To perfect your skill in projection of thought through intense rehearsal in reading aloud a prose selection from the printed page with special attention to phrasing, rhythm, and emphasis.

Length of performance: Seven to ten minutes.

Method and suggestions: We recommend this type of activity for nearly anyone. Children love to be read to—perhaps as much as they enjoy watching television. Others in the family enjoy listening to people read well. The entertainment world has seen successful examples of reading from the public platform during recent years. And some of our outstanding readers, like Charlton Heston, read as part of television programs.

As you prepare this reading, keep the basic skills of reading aloud in mind:

Choice of material—From a current adult magazine, select an article which is primarily expository or descriptive, not narrative, and which, if read well, will be of interest to the audience. Unless otherwise planned, your audience will likely be your classmates and the place your classroom. You may enjoy it more if you meet in the evening and use a small auditorium.

The article should be between 1000 and 1500 words (about 100 lines of print on a book-size page or four or five printed pages).

If your selection is longer, cut it down to a ten-minute length.

Arrangement of material—After you have not more than ten minutes of material ready to read, plan your introductory remarks. Keep your audience in mind as you prepare these remarks. If you have cut out portions of the article in order to get it within the time limits, you may wish to plan some comments to connect the portions that you have chosen to read.

Projection of thought—Since this is not a dramatic reading, your greatest concern is to get meaning across to your audience. Phrasing and emphasis are most important in this process.

Study the material silently to make positively sure that you know the meaning of all the words. Now, find out if you can read it aloud, getting the meaning yourself. Read it to yourself—aloud. Is it easy to group words together as you read or do you read word after word? If you do the latter, you must keep rehearsing it over and over until you read groups of words. Meaning is projected through groups of words, not word by word. Note passages that you do not seem to understand clearly as you hear yourself reading aloud. Do something about those passages. Continue to read them until you hear yourself reading groups of words meaningfully. Or leave out those passages, putting explanatory comments in their place.

Now ask someone to listen to you practice aloud. Ask him to note any words that seem to need more emphasis in order to get the meaning across. Try this: Look at the last paragraph of the article. Read the first sentence aloud. Did your reading seem to bring out the complete meaning of that paragraph as you understand it? Now read the first sentence (or any other that you identify as the topic sentence) of the next to last paragraph. Continue reading one sentence from each paragraph from the end of the article to the beginning. This will force you to read each topic sentence, trying to get the complete meaning of the entire paragraph into your reading. As you continue to practice the selection from beginning to end, try to give emphasis to those sentences you have been studying especially, just as you did in the study exercises.

Projection of emotion—The main thing here is sincerity and earnestness. Have the desire to communicate the idea of the author to the listeners. If there is emotional content, your sincerity and desire will probably help it come through.

Rhythm—Again we recommend a good lively rate for your selection. Do not race with it, but do not be ponderously slow either.

Use pauses. Read an idea briskly, pause, then go on, perhaps at a different rate. Remember that you need not always pause where periods or commas are printed. And sometimes you may wish to pause where no punctuation is printed.

Pronunciation—You must pronounce every word correctly. You are reading the words of another and he is entitled to have his words given correct pronunciation. In your own speeches you might take the liberty of being "folksy," as some very popular television entertainers have done, but when you are reading the words of an author, you do not have that privilege.

Voice control—It is through inflections in pitch and other marks of variety in duration, quality, and intensity that you will bring out the meanings of the selection you are presenting to your audience. You must rehearse to do this. Try recording some of your selection on a tape recorder. Hear it played back. Does it show that you are using a vigorous, energetic presentation? Does it present you as speaking sincerely and earnestly, making the thought of the author predominant? Practice several times with the recorder.

G-4 EVALUATION

Date _____   Student _____

Selection _____   Author _____

Choice of Material	7 6 5 4 3 2 1	*COMMENTS:*	
Arrangement of Material	7 6 5 4 3 2 1		
Projection of Thought	7 6 5 4 3 2 1		
Projection of Emotion	7 6 5 4 3 2 1		
Control of Bodily Activity	7 6 5 4 3 2 1		
Rhythm	7 6 5 4 3 2 1		
Pronunciation	7 6 5 4 3 2 1		
Voice Control	7 6 5 4 3 2 1		

ASSIGNMENT G-5   Reading the Longer Poem Aloud

Aim of assignment: To refine your skills in projection of emotion through intensive rehearsal in reading selected emotional poetry aloud; to achieve listener appreciation; and to consider bodily action, voice control, and rhythm in reading aloud.

Length of performance: Seven to ten minutes.

Method and suggestions: Again we call your attention to the basic skills of oral reading as you make your plans for this performance.

Choice of material—Select a poem or poems that you like. You will profit most if you search for and select something which you have not read aloud before. It may be one long poem or several short ones. Check with your instructor to make sure that you have made a good selection.

Arrangement of material—Whether you choose to read a single long poem or several short ones, you will want to prepare some introductory remarks. These will probably include the titles, authors, background materials, and a word about your plan for the readings.

Projection of thought—First you must understand the thought content of the poem. This is sometimes difficult, because the form of poetry allows—often demands—that word order be inverted. You must know the meaning of each group of words that present a thought. Sometimes that includes less than a line; sometimes more. You should forget "line scheme" and "rhyme scheme."

Read the poem aloud to yourself quietly, searching for meaning. You may need to write a précis to come closer to understanding. Ask your instructor to hear you read it quietly. He will tell you if he understands the meaning as you read.

Projection of emotion—After you have mastered the meaning, you are ready to search out the emotions of each phrase. Identify the emotions of each phrase.

Practice easily and quietly at first. Then as you begin to feel the emotion of the parts of the poem, let out a little. Use more vocal response and bodily action. Put more energy and vitality into the reading. Keep going until you have as much as the poem seems to call for and as much as your audience is likely to accept in the circumstances of the reading—probably your classroom at the class hour.

Control of bodily activity—Remember that you are reading from the printed page. This means that you should stand still. Do not do much acting—not much bodily action, aside from facial gestures plus some shoulder, arm, and hand movement.

If your book is on a reading stand, keep one hand on the page, with your finger on the place, so that when you look back at the text you will find the place quickly. If you hold the book in your hand, do not wave it around. Hold it still. At times it is good to put your free hand on the page. Gesture very little.

Rhythm—Here you have a problem. For too long we have heard children recite poems in a singsong manner dictated by the line and rhyme of the writing. You must break down this rhythm, unless the poem was written with the intention that it should be "sung." Some of the poems of Vachel Lindsay, for example, depend on the rhythm for their effect. Most poetry, however, was written for meaning and for that reason you should read for meaning and let the emotion come out of the meaning, rather than from the form of the writing.

Again, use variety in pausing, speeding up, and slowing down. Ask your instructor to hear you with the purpose of suggesting variety in rhythm. Again, practice with a tape recorder. Consciously try for rhythm changes. Finally, after much practice, use only those rhythm variations that you believe the audience will accept and respond to.

Pronunciation—The first consideration is whether the poem is reflective of the speech of a region or of a dialect of some English-speaking group. If there are regional idiosyncrasies or dialect, find out how to reproduce that type of pronunciation. It may be that no one can help you. In that case, discard that material—or, go ahead and try it, doing the best you can, remembering one thing: your audience must understand what you say, even in dialect.

If there is no specific call for an unusual pronunciation, then be sure you know how to pronounce each word the poet has written—and pronounce it that way.

Voice control—You may enjoy a lot of intensive work here. Mood, feelings, and emotion are best projected through voice quality. Rate, intensity, and pitch are only slightly less important.

Analyze the printed poem and mark it, thought group by thought group, with symbols of your own designed to identify the emotion. Practice each portion aloud, with and without a tape recorder. Then work on the complete selection, trying to get the emotional content of the pages into your voice.

G-5 EVALUATION

Date _____   Student _____

Selection _____   Author _____

Choice of Material	7 6 5 4 3 2 1	*COMMENTS:*
Arrangement of Material	7 6 5 4 3 2 1	
Projection of Thought	7 6 5 4 3 2 1	
Projection of Emotion	7 6 5 4 3 2 1	
Control of Bodily Activity	7 6 5 4 3 2 1	
Rhythm	7 6 5 4 3 2 1	
Pronunciation	7 6 5 4 3 2 1	
Voice Control	7 6 5 4 3 2 1	

APPENDIX

39   Articulation Drills

Everyone profits from articulation drills at some time in his speech training. At the outset, try articulating all the words in the following lists. Then limit your practice to those which are of most value to you. When your instructor makes an inventory of your speech habits, he probably will check certain sounds that are faulty. Practice them, using these lists.

The organization of these words is done on two bases: first they are grouped according to a sound commonly misarticulated, such as [s] [z] [θ] [ð]. Within these groups there are three subdivisions, in most cases. The first presents words wherein the sound comes in the initial position, at the beginning of the word. Next are those words in which the sound is in a medial position. And third, you will find the sound in the terminal position.

[s]	soil	aside	person	dangerous
	solid	baseball	receipt	decrease
said	some	closely	specific	doubtless
sake	soon	concede	wrestler	exerts
sample	south	deceit		goose
sea	sum	erased	across	intense
serve	supreme	gossip	advance	nice
set	sustain	himself	base	produce
sick		innocent	bonus	types
site	absorb	loosed	coarse	voice
social	agency	myself	confess	yes

167

[z]

zany
zeal
zebra
zenith
zephyr
zero
zest
zinc
zinnia
zipper
zircon
zodiac
zone
zoo
Zulu

bazaar
busy
chosen
crazy
desire
easily
magazine
pleasant
praised
prison
result
spasm
stanza
thousand
used
visible
visor

amuse
because
birds
bonds
browse
cabins
chose
clubs
colors
girls
hands
miles
refuse
these
those
was
whose

[ʍ]

whack
whaler

wharf
whatever
wheelbarrow
whenever
whereabouts
whereby
wherefore
wherein
whereof
whereon
wherever
which
while
whimper
whine
whinny
whirlpool
whisk
whither

anywhere
awhile
bewhiskered
everywhere
nowhere
somewhat
somewhere

[w]

wage
wait
wake
wall
war
wash
waste
water
we
wear
week
weight
well
were
wife
will
wind
winter
wisdom
woman
wonder
world

away
awoke
beware
bewitch

downward
glassware
lengthwise
midwinter
Milwaukee
outwit
rewind
seaweed
Southwest
tradewinds
twelve
twenty
twist
underworld
unwelcome
unwise
upward

[θ]

thank
theater
theme
theory
thick
thief
third
thirty
thought
thousand
thread
three
thrift
through
throw

anything
Arthur
authority
Bertha
faithful
Gotham
healthy
marathon
method
nothing
northwest
one-third
sympathy
toothache
twenty-three
wealthy
worthless

both
breath
death
earth

faith
forth
growth
length
month
mouth
north
seventh
south
strength
teeth
tooth
youth

[ð]

than
that
the
their
them
then
there
they
this
those
though
thus

although
another
brother
either
father
feather
further
mother
neither
northern
rhythm
southern
together
within
worthy

bathe
breathe
clothe
lathe
lithe
loathe
scathe
seethe
smooth
soothe
teethe
tithe
with

writhe

[ʃ]

Chicago
shade
shall
shape
she
sheep
shelf
ship
shirk
shoot
shop
short
should
shove
show
shrug
sure

ancient
appreciate
battleship
beneficial
bookshop
direction
education
issue
machinery
official
published
rushing
session
suspicious
threshed

cash
crash
dish
distinguish
English
finish
fish
flourish
foolish
harsh
Irish
marsh
rash
refresh
rush
smash
wash

[ʒ]

azure

casual	chick	junior	Latin	amend
casualty	chief	jury	return	clamor
collusion	child	just	until	empire
composure	chill			example
conclusion	chimney	adjust	bent	foremost
confusion	chop	angel	boat	homely
conversion	chose	budget	bought	improve
decision	chuck	courageous	district	primary
diversion	churn	energy	flat	summary
enclosure		engine	important	
erosion	achieve	forger	not	aim
evasion	coaching	gorgeous	rust	came
exclusion	exchange	injustice	suggest	crime
excursion	marching	intelligent		germ
explosion	matches	major	[d]	him
exposure	merchants	manager		palm
fusion	orchard	object	damp	roam
inclusion	parched	original	day	stem
invasion	purchases	religion	deck	
leisure	reaches	suggested	depend	[n]
measure	richest	unjust	discard	
occasion	teaching		divide	knee
persuasion	touched	acreage	dome	nation
pleasure	watching	advantage	double	near
precision		bridge	during	neck
provision	branch	cottage		neighbor
regime	catch	edge	accident	never
seclusion	clinch	exchange	bender	new
seizure	coach	indulge	broadly	next
transfusion	crutch	knowledge	candy	night
treasure	detach	language	editor	not
version	each	lodge	headline	
vision	etch	page	ladies	annual
	much	pledge	modern	canoe
barrage	peach	range	radio	council
beige	pitch	revenge	sudden	enough
camouflage	porch	siege		envelope
concierge	rich	storage	ahead	final
corsage	search	village	arrested	funny
cortege	such		complied	instance
garage	trench	[t]	expected	leaned
massage	which		ground	many
menage		table	informed	minor
mirage	[dʒ]	tall	period	only
prestige		task	spend	unable
rouge	gem	ten	varied	unlike
sabotage	general	to		
	gypsy	top	[m]	again
[tʃ]	jam	toward		began
	Japan	trust	make	Berlin
chain	jaw	twirl	may	born
chair	jerk		me	confine
chamber	jewel	attack	member	even
chapter	jive	bottom	merry	green
charm	join	captain	mild	lawn
chase	judge	certain	monkey	million
check	judicial	debating	move	ocean
chew	jump	eighteen	my	opinion

position
sustain

[ŋ]

banks
congress
fingers
frank
gangster
Ingersoll
inked
length
Lexington
linger
Long Island
longer
lungs
mangle
rank
single
spangle
strength
sunk
Yankee

along
among
being
bring
carrying
causing
coming
cutting
eating
facing
hang
King
looking
losing
living
making
putting
ring
sang
slung
song
strong
sung
writing
young

[r]

rain
rapid
rate
read
remain
rest
rid
road
rock
rose
rub
ruin

area
arise
arrive
carbine
careen
every
garden
heroic
luxury
narrow
perhaps
prairie
purpose
surprise
terrify
very

are
before
buyer
care
cooler
copper
ever
four
her
hour
labor
lower
paper
pioneer
poor
popular
your

[l]

lack
large
last
laws
lay
leave
leg
life
like
lip
list
live

log
lose
lost
low
lucky

alike
allure
already
believe
below
collar
daily
delicate
fellow
gallop
Holland
privilege
public
value
valve
yellow

appeal
awful
battle
bell
bottle
brittle
cattle
cool
dull
feel
fuel
full
hill
pool
school
small
whole

[æ]

absence
absolute
accident
acid
add
admire
affable
after
algebra
alkali
alley
ambition
animal
answer
apple

aptitude
ashes
ask
aspirin
atlas
atom
avenue
axis

catch
crack
dance
emphatic
fact
fast
financial
gather
handicap
inhabit
ladder
mathematics
natural
package
pant
rang
rapid
placid
sample
scratch
task
travel
valley

[aɪ]

aisle
eyes
I
ice
icicle
Idaho
ideal
identical
idle
Iowa
iron
island
item
ivy
ivory

admire
behind
climate
diagonal
diet
divine
entirely

fighter
likewise
pilot
slightly
wildly
writer

buy
cry
die
dry
fly
fry
high
lie
my
pie
ply
pry
rye
sigh
tie
try

[aʊ]

ouch
ounce
ours
ourselves
outdoor
outer
outfield
outgrow
outguess
outing
outlaw
outlet
outlook
output
outside
owl

about
accountant
astounding
counted
countess
county
doubtless
down
endowment
house
mountain
sound
south
towel
town

allow	boil	alloy	earth	learn
brown	coin	annoy	ermine	nerve
chow	Detroit	boy	irk	person
cow	doily	convoy	Irving	search
endow	embroider	decoy	urban	shirt
how	exploit	deploy	urbane	verse
now	foible	destroy	urge	
plow	hoist	employ	urn	cur
prow	join	envoy		defer
row	joyous	joy	assert	deter
sow	loiter	Roy	bird	err
vow	loyal	toy	circuit	fir
	noise	Troy	concern	her
[ɔɪ]	poison		curve	inter
	rejoice		exert	occur
oil	royal	[ɝ] or [ɜ]	first	purr
oilcloth	soil		flirt	refer
ointment	voice	earliest	further	sir
oyster	void	early	girl	slur
		earn	heard	stir
appoint	ahoy	earnest		

Practice for Accuracy

abolitionist	dandelion	gymnasium	ornithologist
abstracted	decorative	habiliment	ostensibly
accompaniment	defenseless	hallucination	paraphernalia
adjective	delightedly	headquarters	parliamentary
administrative	demonstrative	hippopotamus	pathological
alphabetical	denominational	homogeneous	perpendicular
amidst	descriptive	hypothetical	pessimistic
amongst	deterioration	identification	philanthropic
arithmetic	determinedly	ignominiously	physiognomy
authenticity	dilapidated	imperceptibly	potentiality
bacterial	dishonest	imperturbable	premeditate
bankruptcy	disobedient	incomprehensible	presumptuous
bashfulness	distinguishable	indistinguishable	provocative
beforehand	dramatically	insinuation	psychiatrist
behavior	ecclesiastical	irregularity	psychologically
beneficence	electromotive	journalistic	pyramidal
bibliography	emancipation	justification	quadruped
blessedness	emphatically	kindergarten	querulous
boisterously	enigmatically	kitchenette	radicalism
bystander	extraordinarily	laboratory	ragamuffin
calamity	familiarity	legitimate	recapitulate
candidacy	figuratively	likelihood	recrimination
cannibalism	financially	longitudinal	remunerative
capitalistic	flexibility	luxuriant	reprehensible
carelessly	fraudulent	magnanimity	responsibility
characteristically	generosity	maladjustment	revolutionize
chrysanthemum	genuineness	manufacturer	rigorously
civilization	geographically	marmalade	ruminate
classification	gesticulating	mobilization	sanitarium
coincident	governmental	modernistic	satisfactorily
conciliatory	grammatical	multitudinous	scholasticism
conductivity	gratuitous	necessarily	scientifically
correspondingly	guardianship	nonconformist	sentimentalist

shipbuilding	stalactite	topographical	vocabulary
similitude	surreptitiously	triumphantly	windshield
solicitude	taskmaster	unsophisticated	wretchedness
spiritualism	theologian	utilitarian	zoological

40   *Pronunciation Drills*

Freshman speakers have mispronounced the following words. Have you? Do you?

During the course, pronounce each for some listener. Ask him to check those that you pronounced inaccurately. Check the pronunciations of these words. Learn to say them properly. Use them properly in your speeches.

about	attacked	booklet	certificate	couldn't
absence	attendance	borrowed	chairs	counting
accept	attended	bottle	chances	county
accident	auditorium	bottom	changes	cousin
account	aunt	bought	cheerful	covering
acquainted	auntie	branches	Chicago	cows
acre	author	brass	chocolate	creek
acted	automobile	brick	Christmas	crowded
addition	avenue	bringing	church	current
addresses	average	broken	Cincinnati	cute
adventure	awfully	brothers	cities	cutting
advise	awhile	brought	climate	damage
affectionate	banquet	Buffalo	closed	dances
afternoon	bargain	build	closing	dangerous
afterwards	bath	bureau	cloth	dearest
against	battery	buried	clothes	December
agriculture	battle	business	cloudy	delightful
all right	became	buying	coast	delivered
always	because	calf	coats	dentist
American	been	calling	collar	department
amusement	beginning	calves	collected	depot
amusing	being	can't	colleges	desert
angel	believe	capital	comfort	deserve
another	belongs	captain	common	desk
answer	below	cars	company	Detroit
anybody	belt	case	concert	didn't
apartment	besides	catalog	containing	dies
appreciate	better	catch	conversation	different
April	between	cattle	correct	direction
arithmetic	beyond	caught	costs	dirty
arrived	biggest	cause	costume	disappoint
asked	bird	ceiling	cottage	discovered
athletics	birthday	certainly	cotton	disease

dishes	favorite	hardest	managers	parade
district	February	hardly	manners	paragraph
divided	feed	hasn't	manual	parcel
division	fencing	hated	manufacture	pardon
dogs	fifth	haven't	many	parties
don't	figures	height	mass	passed
doors	filed	history	material	patience
double	filling	holds	matter	patient
doubtful	finally	hole	meaning	pattern
down	find	hospital	measure	payments
dozen	finished	hour	medicine	penmanship
drawing	fished	houses	meeting	perfectly
due	fishing	however	members	perfumes
dumb	fitted	hundred	mention	perhaps
duties	followed	hunting	metal	perspiration
duty	foreign	husband	mighty	photograph
easily	forest	ice cream	milk	physical
Easter	forever	idea	Minneapolis	piano
eating	forget	I'll	minutes	picture
education	fortune	I'm	mischief	Pittsburgh
effort	forty	imagine	mischievous	places
eggs	forward	immediately	model	planted
eighty	fountain	important	moment	playing
election	friend	including	mostly	pleasant
electric	from	increase	mountains	pleasure
elementary	funeral	industry	mouth	pneumonia
eleven	furniture	instant	must	poems
enclose	further	instead	national	poor
engineer	games	institute	natural	popular
English	garage	instrument	nearest	population
enjoying	gasoline	interested	necessary	position
enter	gather	interesting	needed	possible
entered	geography	invite	neglect	posture
entertainment	gentlemen	isn't	nephew	potatoes
entrance	get	January	new	pouch
envelope	gift	just	New Orleans	pound
equipment	giving	kept	newspaper	powder
escape	glad	kindergarten	New York	practice
especially	glasses	kindest	northern	president
et cetera	going	kindle	noted	pretend
evenings	golden	kindness	notice	pretty
everything	good-by	knew	occupied	primary
example	good-night	knowledge	officer	private
excellent	gotten	language	often	probably
excepting	government	larynx	oldest	problems
exchanging	grandfather	laughing	once	produce
excitement	grass	learned	opening	professor
exercises	greatest	length	operate	program
exhibit	greetings	lesson	opinion	property
expected	grievous	liberty	opposite	quarrel
experience	grown	library	ordering	question
experiment	guilty	lining	organized	rabbits
express	habits	literature	ours	railroad
factories	half	little	ourselves	raising
fallen	Halloween	loaded	outside	rather
families	handkerchiefs	Los Angeles	packages	reached
farm	handled	luncheon	painted	realize
farther	hanging	making	palace	reason

recently	secret	suggest	treated	Wednesday
reception	secretary	superintendent	truly	western
refuse	selected	support	truth	what
regular	sell	suppose	Tuesday	whatever
remember	sends	surprise	twelfth	wheat
represent	separate	sweater	twentieth	wheel
requested	settlement	sweetest	twenty	whenever
resort	several	swimming	typewriter	where
respectfully	signature	system	understanding	wherever
returning	since	telegraph	university	whether
ring	sixth	terrible	unpleasant	which
roof	sixty	text	unusual	while
room	skating	Thanksgiving	used	white
route	snowing	theater	usual	why
rural	something	themselves	valuable	with
safest	somewhere	thirty	victory	without
salary	south	thousand	village	witness
sample	spend	thousands	violin	women
San Francisco	spirit	thrown	visited	wonderfully
satisfied	stationery	tickled	visitor	world
Saturday	stomach	tired	waited	wouldn't
saying	student	together	wanting	writer
scheme	studying	tomorrow	wash	yellow
schoolhouse	subjects	tournament	watched	yesterday
science	suddenly	treasure	water	your
Seattle	suffering		wedding	you're

Index

73

P 587